FIVE AGES

FIVE AGES

PROSE POEMS BY

Cassandra Atherton

Oz Hardwick

Paul Hetherington

Paul Munden

Jen Webb

authorised theft

Five Ages
authorised theft / Recent Work Press
Canberra, Australia

This chapbook series was produced with the support of
International Poetry Studies (IPSI), based within the Centre
for Creative and Cultural Research, Faculty of Arts and Design,
University of Canberra.
http://ipsi.org.au

ISBN 978-0-6451808-3-1

Cover image by Caren Florance

recentworkpress.com

RECENT
WORK
PRESS

The AUTHORISED THEFT series of poetry chapbooks was initiated by International Poetry Studies (IPSI) based in the Faculty of Arts and Design at the University of Canberra. The first collection of chapbooks—Cassandra Atherton's Pegs, *Paul Hetherington's* Jars, *Paul Munden's* Keys, *Jen Webb's* Gaps *and Jordan Williams'* Nets—*resulted from discussions connected to IPSI's Prose Poetry Project, inaugurated by IPSI in late 2014. A second collection,* The Taoist Elements, *followed in 2016; a third,* Colours, *in 2017; and a fourth,* Prosody, *in 2018. A fifth series,* The Six Senses, *followed in anthology form in 2019 and, in 2020, the sixth collection, also in anthology form, was entitled* C19: Intertext || Ekphrasis. *This year's anthology has also been produced in the same spirit of collaborative creativity, and includes Oz Hardwick as a new member. IPSI supports and promotes collaborative and collegiate poetic work in a variety of forms, and encourages the collaboration of poets with other artists, such as Caren Florance who has designed the series.*

Hesiod's Five Ages

Paul Hetherington

This seventh collection of AUTHORISED THEFT chapbooks develops a broadly collaborative project that has seen the creation of a considerable number of prose poems. The chapbook series began in 2015 as five small, standalone publications, each containing 21 prose poems on various connected topics, and it has continued ever since. From 2019, the chapbooks have been incorporated into a single, annual anthology—for ease of publication and reference. Until 2020, the five poets involved were Cassandra Atherton, Paul Hetherington, Paul Munden, Jen Webb and Jordan Williams. There were four poets involved last year, when Jordan was unable to take part, and this year Oz Hardwick joined the group. We have taken Hesiod's five ages as our broad theme, with each poet choosing one of these 'ages' as their topic: the golden age, the silver age, the bronze age, the heroic age and the iron age.

In the eighth century BCE, Hesiod—more-or-less a contemporary of Homer, and traditionally represented as a farmer in the Boeotian region of archaic Greece—wrote *Works and Days*, a relatively short epic or didactic poem of 828 lines. Importantly, Hesiod is as much a literary construction as a real person, given that his biography is derived from the works that now bear his name—which, as Zoe Stamatopoulou writes, 'both ancient and modern readers have considered a *nomen loquens*' (2017: 2), or speaking name, rather than the actual name of the author. This is not surprising in the literary context of the archaic Greek world where, as Glenn W Most states, there was 'no tradition of public autobiography', to the extent that 'Hesiod is the first poet of the Western cultural tradition to supply us even with his name, let alone with any other information about his life' (2006: xviii). Stamatopoulou comments:

> The 'autobiographical' passages within Hesiodic poetry present the narrator as a shepherd who was transformed into a poet by the Muses on Mount Helicon . . . we learn that the speaker is the son of a man who migrated from Aeolian Cyme to Ascra, a wretched Boeotian town, in order to avoid poverty . . . We also hear that he had a dispute with his brother, Perses, which was overseen by corrupt local authorities. (2017: 2)

Hesiod is a sophisticated poet despite some of his rustic themes and Richmond Lattimore says of *Works and Days* that:

> Often it suggests itself as the single work, evoked by a particular occasion, of an amateur poet who was really a farmer. But this was not exactly the case. Hesiod had already been to Euboia to compete, with a poem, at the funeral games of Amphidamas ... and had won a prize. (1965: 4)

Works and Days is well known for a number of reasons, including for providing early versions of the Prometheus and Pandora stories (Hesiod's *Theogony* contains the earliest versions) and for its outline of the five ages already mentioned. It was important in the ancient world because, as Hugo H Koning states, 'In a way comparable to Homer and his poems, Hesiod and his works constituted a "fixed standard of reference" for all Greeks' (2010: 8). Hesiod was not the only ancient writer to divide human history into various ages and, notably, in the 'western' tradition, Ovid's famous account of the four ages in his *Metamorphoses* draws on Hesiod's categorisation.

In Hesiod's understanding, humankind has long been in decline, although with some qualifications along the way. The golden age—and I will use Lattimore's persuasive translation—'lived as if they were gods,/ their hearts free from all sorrow,/ by themselves, and without hard work or pain' (1965: 31). In contrast, the silver age was a serious comedown, during which 'A child was a child for a hundred years,/ ... kept at home,/ a complete booby./ But when it came time for them to grow up/ and gain full measure,/ they lived for only a poor short time' (33). The bronze age is characterised by greater vigour but, disturbingly, these people 'came from ash spears' and 'were terrible/ and strong, and the ghastly/ action of Ares was theirs, and violence' (35).

The heroic age contains a 'wonderful generation of hero-men, who are also/ called half-gods' but they are afflicted by 'evil war and ... terrible carnage', even if some 'have their dwelling place,/ and hearts free of sorrow/ in the islands of the blessed' (37). Finally, Hesiod rather regretfully reflects on his own iron age, where 'never by daytime/ will there be an end to hard work and pain,/ nor in the night/ to weariness' (39)—although he does state that 'there shall be some good things/ mixed with the evils' (39). In a number of respects, the iron age sounds like modernity, in which 'one man shall seek the city of another' and 'The vile man will crowd his better out, and attack him with twisted accusations and swear an oath to his story' (41).

As with the chapbooks written in previous years, the broad theme of five ages is understood by all contributors merely as a starting point for often lateral reflections and imaginative forays. In this case, we are not so much interested in history—although various historical references and interpretations are included—but in how contemporary perspectives may re-inflect, challenge and even subvert Hesiod's various statements, assumptions and ideas. Some of the works in this volume castigate and confront contemporary life in stark and uncompromising terms; others are suggestively lyrical; some rewrite literary or folktale traditions; and some engage in cross-cultural journeys and conversations. There are prose poems of considerable pathos or surrealistic inventiveness, meditations on the quotidian, and blunt incursions into very contemporary topics and issues. Koning eloquently points out that 'the past is created in the present' (2010: 3) and, in this case, the present is also created on foundations from the past.

I invite you to enjoy the works in the spirit in which they are offered—as sometimes salutary works about what it is like to experience the twenty-first century while also reflecting on poetic, political, social and historical issues that reach back to important ancient stories and ideas.

Works Cited

Hesiod 1965 *The Works and Days, Theogony, the Shield of Herakles* (transl Richmond Lattimore), Ann Arbor, MI: The University of Michigan Press

Koning, Hugo H 2010 *Hesiod: The Other Poet. Ancient Reception of a Cultural Icon*, Leiden and Boston: Brill

Most, Glenn W 2006 'Introduction', in Glenn W Most (ed and transl), *Hesiod: Theogony, Works and Days, Testimonia*, Cambridge, MA: Harvard University Press, xi–lxxv

Stamatopoulou, Zoe 2017 *Hesiod and Classical Greek Poetry: Reception and Transformation in the Fifth Century BCE*, Cambridge: Cambridge University Press

Patterns of History
Jen Webb

This year we have turned to an ancient myth to produce five sets of poems based on Hesiod's 'The Five Ages' of what is widely translated as 'Man' (Hesiod 2006 [c.700 BCE]). Hesiod's pattern of history is represented almost exclusively in terms of men's experiences. In the few lines committed to the Five Ages (lines 109–201), there is no mention of women in the Golden Age; the idea of mother is mentioned in the Silver Age; nothing in the Bronze Age; a passing reference to 'rich-haired Helen' in the Heroic Age sequence; and at the end of the Iron Age, the goddesses Aidos and Nemesis 'forsake mankind to join the company of the deathless gods'.

It's a history of men, but not one that celebrates the male of the species, and a similar vision emerges across the ancient texts, with Ovid (2001 [c.8 CE]: Book 1.89–150) reiterating Hesiod's account in his *Metamorphoses*. He similarly characterises history's patterns in terms of four metals of diminishing value and increasing hardness: gold, silver, bronze and iron. Other world cultures too focus on men rather than women; and again depict the pattern of history as one of change and decline (Cairns 1971). For philologist David Adams Leeming, this is the standard script. 'Many creation myths', he writes, 'regardless of basic type, tell the story of the failed creation or the fall of humanity' (2010: 2). We—male humans, at least—begin history in the company of the gods. Then, through violence, venality or impiety, we end by slugging it out in a disenchanted world of diminishing peace, wisdom and justice.

This bleak philosophy of human progress as decline (Archembauld 1966) is countered by a far more optimistic view that begins, arguably, with the European Enlightenment. Thomas Huxley's *Evidence as to Man's Place in Nature* (1863), for instance, includes a frontispiece that presents a sequence of skeletons who move across the page, changing from 'primitive' to 'sophisticated'. A different but related graphic appears in the much-parodied March of Progress, Rudolph Zallinger's 1965 visual argument that traces a steady 'improvement' in humans: from hunched ape through clumsy Neanderthal to sophisticated, and vertical, modern man. As James Shreeve observes, the effect of this graphic is that 'You watch humanity unfold like a flower, each ancestor the ripened promise of the one that came before' (1995: 13): a sense of improvability that lives on in a Steven Pinker-style insistence that history just keeps getting better (Pinker et al. 2016).

Poetry enters the story not only because that is where it starts, with Hesiod et al., but also because poetry is an artform committed to world-making. It is not poetry's responsibility to make an argument for one or other story of origin, or to lay out a philosophy of history, but poetry is an art practice that is imbued with the capacity to report on, and represent, the world. In his *Der Meridian*, Paul Celan discussed poetry and world, and writes, 'the poem is born dark: the result of a radical individuation, it is born as a piece of language, as far as language manages to be world, is loaded with world' (in Joris 2005: 5). It is the world-weight of language that we five poets have explored in this sequence of poems. From the dreams of gold and its affordances, through to the monstrous masculinity of iron-men, the sequences explore ways of seeing and being that interrupt the notion of progress of history. The poets' perspectives align with Roland Barthes' definition of myth—that it is *'a type of speech'* (Barthes 1972: 107, emphasis in original)—and picks various paths through such questions as: what speech?; what is spoken?; and, who speaks?

Works Cited

Archambault, Paul 1966 'The Ages of Man and the Ages of the World: A Study of Two Traditions', *Revue d'Etudes Augustiniennes et Patristiques* 12, no.3-4 (1966), 193–228.

Barthes, Roland 1972, *Mythologies* (transl Annette Lavers), New York, NY: Farrar, Straus & Giroux

Cairns, Grace 1971 *Philosophies of History: Meeting of East and West in Cycle-Pattern Theories of History*, New York, NY: Citadel Press

Hesiod 2006 [c.700 BCE] *Theogony, Works and Days, and The Shield of Heracles* (transl Hugh Evelyn-White), New York, NY: Dover Publications

Joris, Pierre 2005 *Selections: Paul Celan*, Berkeley, CA: University of California Press

Leeming, David 2010 *Creation Myths of the World: An Encyclopedia* (2nd edn), Santa Barbara, CA: ABC–CLIO Books

Ovid 2001 [c.8 CE] *The Metamorphoses* (transl Horace Gregory), New York, NY: Signet

Pinker, Steven, Matt Ridley, Alain de Botton, and Malcolm Gladwell 2016 *Do Humankind's Best Days Lie Ahead?* New York, NY: Simon & Schuster

Shreeve, James 1995 *The Neandertal Enigma: Solving the Mystery of Modern Human Origins*, New York, NY: William Morrow and Company

Zallinger, Rudolph 1965 'The Road to Homo Sapiens', in *Early Man*, New York, NY: Time-Life Books

THE GOLDEN AGE

PAUL HETHERINGTON

'I did not know that mankind were suffering for want of gold. I have seen a little of it. I know that it is very malleable, but not so malleable as wit. A grain of gold will gild a great surface, but not so much as a grain of wisdom.'

—*Henry David Thoreau*

The Golden Age

We imagined being in the golden age, fire climbing across mountain firs like a passage out of Homer—until rain washed us with palpitating hands. We marshalled the fire's glimmering rubies with branches but, tiring of the fantasy, walked back to the hotel, looking over oyster beds in the bay. On your canvases fruit blossomed in strange colours; late afternoon washed our walls in Burnt Sienna. Delight; exquisite feeling; an abandonment of time over succeeding, wanton days. You hid in the old museum's shadows where Greek spears and shields lined the walls, as I tried to find you, tantalised by willed delay. Then, walking downstairs in our contemporary clothes, we sensed time's smear. I failed to find your intimate glance. You were Demeter descending to unknown places— remote, chiselled, unspeaking; a persona in a golden mask.

Midas

My cutlets are unchewable gold; my daughter an unkissable object; my jewels and pearls turn to metal; roses are stiff in the garden—even my ears are stained yellow. But my sadness grows monstrous. What I possess will be melted and my fluent rhetoric clatter like coin. Yet, though I'd show contrition—my advisors urge me to pray—I can't resist my games: touching lavish banquets; grasping art my painters present (and even the painters); pushing a child's pram; stroking slave girls in their beds. All this I anoint—and my pride in myself compounds. To transform the world; to leave others forever mid-sentence; to stifle the yawn of a nurse; to quell my advisors' speeches—that pleasing diminuendo of talk. It's almost perfect—and all Apollo has left me. Even my hunger departs. I am goldsmith and king at once.

Alchemy

The three of us bought all the lead from the scrap yard. We melted and coddled it for days, adding and subtracting, until finally gold began to show—small hints of it, like speckles on an egg. After four more days, a long streak like an exclamation. We watched that widen, like a smile, or a suitcase full of banknotes being opened. We stuck to the instructions—discussing the medieval grave where they'd been found, crossing ourselves. And, barely believing, we saw gold bloom in the molten lead like an absurd creature—radiating with spokes, lustred like late afternoon's sleepiest sunshine. We danced before the cauldron, sang hymns and shanties, opened a magnum of champagne. 'Five more hours,' you said as the unexpected downpour started; as the shed's roof began to leak and water fizzed on molten metal. After ten minutes we'd jerry-rigged a shield but, stepping back, saw only a grey and writhing turbulence. Afterwards, no-one took us seriously—and we'd hardly have believed it ourselves except for the one spoon you'd dipped. It ladled a shine of gold like the promise of permanent feasting.

Au

The symbol might have meant Australia before the invention of dollars, or the cry made by an exotic species of bird when encountering early European explorers— 'stay away'. Now it symbolises a 'safe haven' from crashing stock prices—something you might heavily hold in hands next to a security deposit box, wondering what your life weighs—surely not these bars of yellow metal. Impurities are extracted until all that's left is density and colour coveted by the security guard. It's without obvious character, though it conjures the colour of deep afternoon sunshine when you were a child hiding next to an oleander—pushing your feet against sandal straps, wanting to run down the road. But something was holding you there—a sense of belonging to those minutes; a fascination with the way your skin gathered heat like an extended caress; a weight of new, obdurate thought: 'This moment is gold'.

Seventy-nine

The number of Mr Mack's house, who had lived in the street for thirty-eight years, squeezing caterpillars from his garden's leaves and pushing shiny prongs into soil, like a suburban inquisitor. He'd never married, saying 'why would you waste your time with a woman', as if that was his last word on the subject, sliding girly magazines under his couch on the day you visited to pick up jars of jam. That was his love—stirring apricots and plums picked from weighed-down trees, steeping kernels to extract the flavour. He sold them for four dollars a jar and, although no-one liked him, his jam was exquisite. You wanted to learn how to make preserves and your mother said, 'he's harmless enough', so you found yourself next to his stove as he placed slices of home-grown lemons in a saucepan. The resulting gold marmalade was a strange blessing of flavours, making morning toast into a definition of piquant-sour-sweetness—as if sun had entered the stickiness, or a god distilled an impossible fruity attar. 'He's a real creep', you said, but your mother put the laden toast in her mouth and shut her eyes.

Acid Test

The Chemistry teacher defined it for the class—'rub gold on black stone and apply nitric acid.' You imagined the resistant mark that signalled precious ore; thought of carting a wrapped nugget to safety in a horse's saddle and of the wealth it would bring. You considered your poor grades and reports of your bad attitude. You remembered overhearing your teacher talking about his son's addiction—'I gave him every chance and he simply failed the acid test.' You decided you'd reform, writing a life plan in the back of an exercise book, envisioning yourself becoming a metallurgist at the age of twenty-five and buying a large oceanfront house. It might have happened if you'd not lost your friend. Now you're making new meaning, memorialising those boys' lives in poems—the one who died; the one who died with him.

Lead

The one alchemy you desire is your daughter's love, despite
a decade of darkening anger and reproach. A deep wish
and crucible in which you throw memory's lead weights
and the truths you've sworn by—and handfuls of anxiety.
Yet her accusations are too plentiful and you barely
remember events she recounts—as if reading a torn recipe
and missing key ingredients. You heat and stir; debate
terms; examine books that claim to have the method. You
utter a variety of spells and throw coins in wishing wells,
hoping that next time gold will show through. One day
there's a hint—a bubbling of long-distance affection—but
the next day the gold's gone, base metal staring back like
a frown.

California Dreaming

Taking poverty by the scruff of the neck, panning and crevicing, levering with screwdriver and spoon, hammering and chiselling. Supping on moonshine and visiting 'cat houses' where women keep guns under mattresses. Preaching the credo—'God will make riches for those with gilded dreams.' Air running through tents and huts is ghosted by ideas of bungalows—and outdoors living: hiking, shooting black bears, hauling trout, being-in-the-sun. Every best notion of unreality grows: Hollywood, vineyards, the dotcom boom. And still George and Lennie retell their story, dreaming of a farm and soft fur. Curley's wife's nails are red—his jealousy flickers. Crooks' gold-rimmed glasses watch a spoiled world.

Archaeologist

He found the burial with its gold ornaments in shapes
prized by that ancient culture—a small llama, a sun disc,
a serpentine necklace, a ceremonial mask, some trinkets.
Also bones, dispersed a little, of what were presumably
mother and child. High rank, he thought, as far as that
might be judged, wondering whether the girl played as his
own daughters did; whether the trinkets were her toys;
whether Spanish smallpox killed her—or a conquistador's
murderous work. He knew many were buried; that the
killing had been efficient. He yearned for a time capsule—
to go back where gold was smithed and fashioned as this
woman and child expressed amazement. He thought of the
centre of the earth—Cusco; and how every consciousness
homes in on what it knows. Looking at the verdant land-
scape, he imagined the woman bringing home grain;
saw the constellations she witnessed; wondered at their
cycling immensity. He conjured his last view of Lake
Titicaca. Sounds resonated—an ancient, deep lament; a
clanking lust.

Rumiñawi

You can hear it in the Llanganates Mountains—Pizarro's
ghost, carrying sword and lance, complaining about the
lost Inca treasure and cursing the name of Rumiñawi.
His eyes search every ridge and river as his spirit travels
between the Andes and Amazon. Gold and silver pile
up in rooms and, again, he melts every precious object—
artworks, artefacts and decorations. Imperturbably
lustrous and stripped of beauty, the stacked gold bars
are shipped away. Yet, in thrall to a dream of perpetual
conquest, Pizarro tortures and murders Rumiñawi again.
The Inca general looks back at gold's relentless stare.

Gold Medal

Or, faux gold, with the teacher bending to place it around her neck with his usual unctuous smile, while her muscles ache from the sprint—one flurrying 50-metre length of the pool and her stretching touch a few millimetres ahead of Melissa. They'd been best friends, with Melissa the 'possible state champion' and her own efforts praised as 'determined'. The teachers were already talking about a wild card entry for Melissa into the interschool carnival, and the head coach casually asked her if she'd give up her place because 'your friend was out-of-sorts'—though her own time was a school record. 'No,' she said simply, the word flying out of her mouth like a stinging insect. Later, she beat Melissa again, who was soon enrolled at a different school. A year later at the state trials she touched out Melissa by a fingernail. That gold was heavy on her skin, their old intimacy a shining, inert idea.

Goldfish

To and fro, the strangest entities, as if seen through a window—finning through grotto and long weed; past the pirate's chest, around the seated skeleton and broken ship's hull. My childhood also looked through window glass, feeling sunlight as incursions, struck by a childish wish for change. Back and forth from low primary school buildings, reading Biggles adventures in the library, imagining myself a Royal Flying Corps scout—but, even at eleven, wearying of the relentless derring-do. A boy invited me to see his goldfish, circling a large tank—returning, and returning in startling yellows, greens and oranges like a hallucinated vision of the tropics. And a single fish dressed in gold that passed and vanished. I stood waiting for it to return, searching the tank, until summoned home.

Golden Syrup

A river boat heaves upriver, diesel fumes climbing and settling all morning, while you stare over the handrail at landscape and sky, imagining yourself Marlowe in the extraordinary jungle. But, here, there are tamed trees and fields; a vista to further unsettle your longing. You disembark for the museum tour and, on the way home, as rapids make the boat bounce, one of the crew brings a plate of steaming pancakes, cooked in brown butter and teetering with a slow spread and slide. On the chill afternoon, with a damp breeze climbing your shirt, you spear one after another, the yellow-dark taste uplifting in your mouth like the return of something forgotten— hearing yourself yelling as an eleven-year-old, pushing past your siblings to gather soft, flat cakes, wondering at the transmutation of gold.

Wire

A wire of a single atom's width—and still it stretches. You didn't believe it possible until someone showed you a magnified image. And its strange stability fascinates— you think of self being infinitely elongated; of a deity made from beaten sheets as wide as the sky. You imagine semi-transparent gold providing a lens for viewing celestial spheres—each nesting and revolving in their own quintessence. It's an absurd fantasy, yet gold seems to insist on the marvellous and grotesque. You imagine the world's wired and unwired connections as unseen and infinite golden strands; of rhetoric and poetry as golden forms of speech. You imagine your lover dressed in shimmering gold leaf. You peel it from her body and she dissolves into exquisite modes of caress.

Ring

It sat like a miniature, jewelled Tower of Babel, as if it might climb all the way to heaven from her middle finger. When she held a glass of wine, it was all angles and glints, the old, yellow gold casting a 24-karat shine into deepening afternoon. Whatever she handled seemed to climb into the ring—so that cooking translated aromas as if they were funnelled toward the sky; and perfumes were expressed in motions of her hand. We touched tentatively, and I imagined that structure of precious gems roaming over my skin, as if a builder was finding a place to lay her tower down; or a restless, golden insect was suddenly all eyes. Occasionally, as her hands rested near me, the diamond point reminded me of our incipient separation. Yet, she built emotions that might be towers; a whole city of exclamation, founded on golden, lassitudinous evenings and heights we climbed.

Diamond Ring

Gold diamond ring, refashioned, shaped, and held on her reaching hand. Feelings like squid on an ocean floor, wrapping movement in their forward-sidling progress. This love like the embrace of a small room, in which walls are pressed by a rolling spine; in which talk becomes language's staccato eruptions. You read it on your vertebrae; you're the dissolution of stubborn thought. The room leans and breathes with the fog of centuries; there are no pertinent elsewheres. Gold appears to merge with skin; diamonds are impeccable droplets about to fall. We're sea creatures searching the floor, stuttering back toward articulate speech.

Golden Apples of the Sun

After WB Yeats

I didn't feel old, or much of a wanderer, but had been to the mind's hollow and uncomfortable places. I thought of plucking heads of grass and kissing a young woman, feeling time's dissolution like a kind of weather, uncertain about what I cared for. She embraced me and held a kiss, saying we were parting. Sappy stalks harried my legs and grass heads were dry between my fingers. I never wanted to know where she went, my words failed to encompass our feeling—even now, when memory drags forty years through mind. She handed me a book, quoting a line about golden apples, but I missed the reference, being callow and moon-silvered.

The Frog Prince

For CA

He wouldn't take no for an answer, especially after he'd retrieved my golden ball so punctiliously. I'd thrown him against the wall and he'd morphed into that conceited prince who smelt of pond weed. His servant, Henry's three iron bands snapped from around his heart and he, too, was released into ardour—but for his master rather than me. The awkward threesome was a real pain until I agreed to marry him—because it's a truth universally acknowledged that a single woman without money must want a prince. Which wasn't true, but it sounded plausible when he first said it to me over a glass of wine—and, in any case, it was the eighteenth century so my options were strictly limited. He told me he had a wide *demesne*, but it proved mainly marshland and a few straggly waterways, so we built a houseboat and lived like paupers, and before long I had his little frogs to look after—he hadn't told me that despite his metamorphosis all he could produce were jelly-like spawnings. And I'd tell you the moral, except he told me not to write it down.

Rumplestiltskin

That was the first absurdity—that I'd believe he had a ridiculous name even though he looked like any Johnny-come-lately who wanted to bed me just for helping out with a few chores. But apparently it was his Twitter handle—and he claimed his real name was Sebastian (I laughed for minutes, having already seen the Evelyn Waugh novel sticking out of his manbag). Actually, the first absurdity was the idea that he might spin my straw into gold, because everyone knows that was a metaphor. The king who'd locked me away was simply trying to force me to go where I never would willingly—the long jumper he was wearing was the real giveaway. So, I said 'yes, why not have a go' and he sat at the treadle puffing and complaining while I got some really fabulous chemical dye and, next morning, told the king that it may not be gold but it sure looked good. The king smiled and ordered Rumplestiltskin evicted. He said 'You can't even guess my name', and I said, 'Well, Rumplestiltskin literally means "little rattle stilt", and that sounds right after all'—and despite some kicking and swearing, it was the last I heard of him. When the king proposed, I told him to forget his gender-binary assumptions, wedding my favourite princess instead. Her straw was blonde as morning and I put my spindle away.

The Goose that Laid the Golden Eggs

It wasn't anything to do with greed, although my husband put that story about afterwards because somehow it sounded better than the truth. And we'd already hoarded many of the golden eggs and were living comfortably. My husband said 'Never admit it', but I had to get it out—we both hated that smarmy, self-satisfied bird. In the old days, birds could talk and this one preened herself with appalling views—she praised the cruel, orange-haired king; said birds were far-and-away the superior species; and insisted, if we wanted her eggs, that I devote all my time to her. What's more, she regularly made a mess of our library as only an overfed bird could. One day we clubbed her to death because we hated that feathered tyranny. And, to be honest, we were sick of the eggs. The gold was riddled with rotten opinions.

Jack and the Beanstalk

It's a very old story: how I climbed the beanstalk and stole the giant's most valuable possessions, including a bag of gold (which my parents converted to valuable shares), a goose that laid golden eggs (they sold her off for a tidy profit) and a harp that played by itself (they loved that despite its sentimental repertoire). There were other irritants, too, and I wanted to go back to the giant's world, but outside the window the slashed beanstalk was withered and that literary giant—he was always quoting one book or another—had fallen to his death. My parents were suspicious of 'poncy' culture, liking nothing more than a good public hanging, and I realised what I'd destroyed. One afternoon I took my parents' best cow to market and procured more beans, throwing them on the ground. The next morning, baking the last of the beans for breakfast, I watched tendrils writhe skyward. Adventure sang like an opera.

THE SILVER AGE

OZ HARDWICK

'I am silver and exact. I have no preconceptions.
Whatever I see I swallow immediately
Just as it is, unmisted by love or dislike.'

—*Sylvia Plath, 'Mirror'*

Typo

It began with a typo—the accent of Everest—but now she feels obliged to speak in snow-capped stone, too vast for her lovers to comprehend. Even her intake of breath is heroic Reich propaganda, eroded by eighty years into numinous homo-eroticism, where two fresh-faced muscular youths fear to stop climbing, lest they fall to uncontrollable humping in a bivvy bag, oblivious to the blonde-plaited Grail-Maiden descending from a dazzling sunset. And when she breathes out, there's Tom Cruise, arcing into oblivion like a goat on a bungee, rescuing all of the aforementioned from Romantic transcendence, the Sublime, and, where applicable, the burning shame of unmanliness. In her shadow, I'm an overweight miner celebrity, resuscitating my airless fame for unspecified charities, shovel in hand, digging deep into the mountain's roots.

The Silver Age

We made the journey in sensitive light, smart as crystals, silver trickling from soft play and all parameters permeable. We invaded compounds, accrued compound interest, and compounded our irreversible changes with a bath of hypo. For every action there is an equal and opposite reaction: sometimes it's a smile and sometimes it's an outstretched, flapping palm, flat as a bat. Grain takes on its own beauty, so we settle and become farmers, nurturing areas of graduated shadow into pure pattern. Beauty is deep as skin and spreads itself on billboards the size of buildings. We manufacture rudimentary tools to capture fleeting certainties and to differentiate ourselves from the crows that gather in waving wheatfields which are running to seed. From here on in, it's all dreams and dances, primping our rig for carpets that we know to be red, even though we only see black and white. We'll fade with age and carry the light that bleeds from each transgression. The irrefutable laws of physics assure us there's time to change, so we'll no doubt change it for local currency when we run out of wine and spices; then we'll post guards, second class, with no return address. The footprints we left on the Moon are still there, bathed in silver light.

Coming of Age

A century of childhood behind tinted windows / a concrete memorial to soft play / a balsa plane downed in the road / a bear with no voice / a VHS tape tangled in the machine. We have reached the third of five imaginary towns we must traverse on the road to where we were never meant to be, and we circle the wagons for the indecisive fight that's just part of the deal. We're making good time from the finest ingredients, storing it in sealed jars that we wrap in outgrown school uniforms to keep it from the light; and we're making poor excuses from rose petals and tap water, dabbing them behind our ears to ward off growing old. We've a bonfire of weathervanes and 20/20 vision, and the capricious flames illuminate dazed faces, flat against green glass / dust sealed in white scars / running feet in loose, scuffed shoes / picture books that cry and sing / reels of magnetic tape wiped clean as noses. When the ashes cool, we'll kick over the traces, load up our carts and carabines, and cross the line between irreconcilable differences.

The Summons

A courier brings salmon on a silver platter and an invitation from the Queen. It's a card with fluted edges, printed by hand, and my connoisseur fingers delight in the subtle variations in depth of each letter. When I stroke the surface lightly there's the scent of tangerines and bright sapphires, with the hint of a long case clock in a darkened study, and when I hold it to my ear I hear cutlery laid out with military precision and a child sleeping in a small boat. The evening demands formulaic dress, so I select a suit from a celebrity wedding and dust the colour from its collar until it's almost invisible. For my *plus one* I accompany my reflection in a silver spoon, careful not to meet each other's eye lest we collapse into giggles. A man in silk britches and a tricorn hat rings in the future we've been promised every evening on the news, and a pumpkin drawn by white mice waits at the kerb. When I leave the house, my key doesn't fit the lock, and the path stretches for miles through a wood full of wolves and lost orphans. I tell the cat I'll be home by midnight and, whatever hungers may come knocking at the door, not to touch the salmon.

Border Control

Every cloud has a silver bullet. We stack our superstitions one by one, careful not to crack their surfaces, storing them against anticipated disorders. There are traffic disruptions, thematic discontinuities, record tides, and hailstones the size of goose eggs. Naturally, we want to see it all, to post it on social media to prove that it's true, so we load up with wet collodion and flash powder, thick gloves, and sharpened stakes, hanging out of swerving vans like the Keystone Cops, heading for the soft border. Beliefs slide and totter on hairpin bends, hinting at lycanthropy and transubstantiation; but by the time we reach where we thought we were heading, the uncanny has become the new normal, with werewolves in every corner café, howling into mobiles as the signal breaks up like polar ice.

'Border Control' was first published in *Pennine Platform 86* (2019).

Break

Fleeing the crush, feeling the rush, embracing the hush of the drop from a first floor window straight into the best seat in the house—I wear luck like a hand-me-down coat, buttoned up all wrong, with a five pound note sewn into the lining and a wasp in the top pocket. As my phone pings another lottery win, I watch the road and light my exploding cigar. There's a car in the distance that could be a limo or a hearse, with a suited monkey driving and a gun under the seat, and although it's heading the other way, I know it has my heart stabbed into its GPS. My watch speaks in semaphore and the twitch in my eye is Morse code, but neither is to be relied on at times like this, and I trust instead to the voice in my head which tells me I'm lucky, but not that lucky. Crush/rush/hush: my coat flaps in the smoke-edged breeze. At the side of the road is a burning bush and a phone box papered with cards advertising intercession to higher powers. There's a buzzing in my pocket and my phone's dead. My watch has stopped breathing. I carry a silver key, cold on the flat of my tongue.

This Little Piggy

Hands in each other's pockets, blades in each other's backs, crooked smiles painted on all the eggshell faces, and the flutter of the kill in each dark absence of heart. It takes a scalpel to slice to the truth, then it takes a blind man to recognise it and a girl with a split tongue and a stone in her throat to tell it straight or slant. Gatekeepers pitch dice and share the spoils of slaughter, their laughter soiling their starched pants as they pant to a climax of raking claws. An eye no longer quits an eye and teeth are yesterday's currency. Markets have crashed, there are bodies still unaccounted for, and accounts don't add up, as creditors circle the wreckage in their best bibs and tuckers, sharpening their shiny knives. There's nothing in your pocket but planted evidence that grows like a tumour, or a rumour, or a rupture, or an eruption. In the mess and the madness, a hand like a cane lifts the lip of your flimsy defences, and a voice as sticky as albumen oozes from a cracked mask. Someone's taken a shine to you. Someone's taken your shine.

Prescription for the New Cosmology

I lay out my medication like a map of the Solar System, lining up pills on a measured scale, Mars to Uranus, on the kitchen table. Experience has shown me that calm is as much about metaphor as it is about pharmacology, and that increased dopamine neurotransmission in the frontal cortex is no more or less effective than, say, a ladder that stretches from an unkempt flower bed to a cloud that resembles a loosely curled fist. So, I climb the ladder and uncurl the fingers. Inside is a palm crossed with silver lines, like canals glimpsed in moonlight, and I think I see paper boats with paper lanterns, paper birds diving for paper fish. Each of the boats is named after a planet and each of the birds is dust igniting at the edge of the Earth's atmosphere. The hand that holds them all is a serotonin-norepinephrine reuptake inhibitor, the ladder is a telescope with a cracked objective lens, and the flower bed is Pluto, wondering what it did wrong. The kitchen table's just the kitchen table, calmly slipping out of focus.

The Age of Ecdysis

I'm at that age at which I slough my silver skin and leave
my reflection hanging in each mirrored surface from which
I turn away. My walls are a gallery of pokerwork notices
to remind me to eat and sleep, and I set alerts to feed the
cat and take my prescribed medication. On a schedule I
can't follow, the council sends bags for the parts of me I no
longer use, but they never collect them, so they clutter the
step until foxes rip them open to feed their hungry young.
There are fines for feeding foxes and fines for not carrying
photo ID, but my picture is different each time I look: this
morning it was a hand-tinted diorama of a seaside pier
in flames, but more often than not it's a fox caught in a
camera trap as it skitters down the back ginnel, its pelt
prickling silver with unseasonable frost. I'm at that age at
which my diary's full but I don't know what day it is, and
when I need to meet strangers in virtual rooms or open
public spaces, my skin's gone and even my reflection is
trapped inside mismatched hand-me-down teaspoons. A
celebrity whose face I can't place smiles from the TV and
tells me I'm only as old as I feel, but all I feel is tired and
the need to turn away.

The Basho All-Night Diner

In the park, the pond's shrunk to a spoonful of green soup that even the trees won't touch. Someone's laid out lawns like placemats and blackthorn gleams like ranks of polished cutlery, but the kitchen's a cacophony of flung pans and obscenities boiling over. I go there when I can't sleep, sharp as my sister's wedding, dressed to the nines, and a sprig of childhood illness neat in my buttonhole. My credit's good, my good name's creditable, there's dirt beneath my fingernails, and I have my special table that faces a weed-wrapped wall. The maître d' mumbles, his mouth muffled in hatching moths, but there's no need to speak after all this time, and the kitchen's already silent but for the breeze and a distant game of cricket. There's a ripple of applause from the pavilion, a cricket chirps, a breeze ruffles the lawn like an affectionate aunt, and a starched girl brings a tourmaline lake on a silver platter. Silence. Trees bow to drink, pray, or just look at their own reflections. A frog hops/splash/disappears.

Work in Progress

It's the time of year when hands wake up each morning with an itch and a clipboard full of lists: things to make, things to do, and Big Questions to ponder in the slant light. The first is easy, with war and peace available online in self-assembly flatpacks, and love in a pack of sachets half hidden behind the bins. Then I set myself attainable goals, set camera traps to capture foxes, and set cats among pigeons in a purely metaphorical sense, before starting a further list of clichéd phrases to be avoided like the plague. It's a work in progress. Next, I settle in the low sun to consider who first may have turned from a straining table, glut-happy and dazed with perfection, and set down their satisfaction in rhyme or shaded line, siphoning their immortal sleep into dust. Are shadows, I wonder, caged or free; and if I burn my books, will I even know I'm alive? I add *Mistakes* to the 'Make' list and *Incineration* to the 'Do' list and—when my hands wake up tomorrow shaped into birds and rabbits, just like my mother showed me when I was small—I'll wonder whose writing this is and whether or not I should trust them.

The Book of Signs

(after Theophrastus)

It was one of those days on which the sea climbed back into the clouds, on which bird could never be anything but a verb. We were explorers in search of ice, astronauts in search of gravity, musicians in search of every chord we'd ever lost. The weather was flat as a billboard for a closing-down sale, hard as a hospital hand that reaches for the off switch. We found a silver ladder amongst the skins and bottles beneath the pier—each rung ringing with biblical feet, the repetitive tunes of school assemblies, and stacks of shuddering Sundays when every door in the world was locked—and we tossed an old half crown to decide who would climb and who would stay behind to circulate alibis and excuses. I won or lost, leant the cap against salt spray, and clutched the stiles like knives jammed in the hotplate of a condemned bedsit, my palms burning as I watched your bare feet ascending into waves, climbing into birds, disappearing into alibis and excuses.

The Hourglass Arcade

Let sleeping birds fall from the sky. I grip a hand that's made of sand and walk the familiar arcades. There are machines for making friends and fortune tellers on every corner. There are women with their arms full of needles and men who can barely breathe as they stretch low across pool tables. A bird sighting land is worth two under the bus. I cross my own palm with sand and silver, making mirrors from broken glass and flaked paint. There are stalls selling souls and booths to choose new faces. There's a woman with a lantern gathering moths and a man whose speech is bleach to purify the white-tiled walls. I cross off missing items from a list of essential purchases, palming loose change. The easy bird catches the warm air just before it strikes the ground. There are posters advertising luxury breaks and flyers urging uprisings. There's a photo of a woman with a number to contact and a man's name scratched in the callbox glass. I have sand beneath my fingernails and eyelids. Something in the machinery of compassion is broken and my hands flutter like spooked birds.

Aliens

Memory is the light of the moon, with tanks of sour milk waiting on a strange shore. Once there were astronauts passing to and fro, carrying photos of their smiling sweethearts and bringing back dust and stones to amaze schoolkids. Now they just go round and round, cold as a lost lifeboat on a sea of sour milk. Just one small explosion can reshape the universe, blowing nostalgia through the curtains, redirecting streams and leaving tankers queued up on familiar shores. Out of the fridge, milk sours within two hours, tops, and it's 1.26 seconds since this light left the Moon; there are representatives of four space agencies in the iss and any number of nationalities sleeping in stranded cabs, each one dreaming of how their smiling sweetheart looked as they left. The world is warming, memory is cooling, but moonlight's still silver.

Mortality: An Interim Report

More than anything, ghosts want certainty, so when they ask, *Why did we die?* they're not just interrogating cause and effect regarding the impact of years or polished metal, or the breath that catches and drifts away like an accordion sighing to the wistful close of a song about love and drinking; they're looking at that dealer's silver scales, wildly out of whack, with little but losses on either side. It could be the pure stuff—love, dreams, yada yada—but it's ground so fine and cut with so many questions that it could just be sand in shoes from a bus trip to the coast, or grit in an eye that stares from a top floor window at the space left by a departing taxi. From force of habit, they're weighing up the cost, though their pockets are as empty as their beds and mailboxes and, besides, the exchange rate is a neat zero. So, what they want when they ask, *Why did we die?* is less about life and the mechanics of its afterwards, and more about queueing for sweets in a 60s newsagent's, with its lurid paperbacks and its glass-fronted cabinet of fireworks—Scarlet Fury, Stromboli, Harbour Light—and knowing for sure that there was so much more to come.

The Promise

Returning home, the lights are dim, as if someone slackened the spectrum while we were away. Rooms are less tangible, redder and deader, and walls hint at a dull pulse. This, we decide, is what recovery looks like: not a blue dress buttoned on the first day of school; not a posey of violets in a jar by the window; not inked initials in the collar of a stiff white gown, and nothing at all like a blot-blue tarn cupped in the palm of a new-born mountain. From room to room, each lamp we light has a lower wattage than the last, so that by the time we reach the bedroom, the click of the switch plunges us into the infrared. While you fall asleep as soon as you trip, still in your outdoor clothes, onto your side of the bed, I make virtue of necessity and develop all the films that have been half-wound in cameras since the millennium, filling my lungs with vinegar as I feel lost friends and family tingle at my fingertips in gelatin and silver, with their new clothes and their eyes full of school holidays. When the day eventually dawns, I'll frame them like a medieval allegory, and tell you of all their love and in what circumstances they died; but now I'll drape you in a subtle cloth, listen to the light waves murmuring at the foot of the stairs, and wait for the robin, the thrush, the blackbird, the wren, and their whole chaotic chorus to welcome the day.

Epic

Shouting and pointing, no one notices the babe in the basket, bobbing in the storm drain with a silver coin beneath its tongue. There are fat-sailed ships approaching, or maybe even dragons, the fishnet veil ripping to 793 on the Northumbrian coast; there's something unnatural rippling immaculate lawns and turning houses inside out. Why would anyone notice a child with a green snake wrapped around his wrist spinning through the overflow between running legs? It's a day for biblical wailing and rending of garments, for the broad gestures of nineteenth-century etchings and that Cecil B. DeMille choreography of crowds. It's a day for Fritz Lang fear in every startled eye. There's a pile-up of tigers and school buses at every amber light, and bridges swing like skipping ropes, or tripwires triggering a fusillade of IDEs. There's a silver boy walking on the water, a basket on his tipped hip and a green snake beneath his tongue. He knows the spells to pacify dragons and science to still bridges, and he can sing explosions back into birds' nests and cinema queues. Of course, no one notices—why would they?—but maybe they will when the snake grows into a man.

A History of First Dates

Silver hedges dissect the vegetable night that grows around us like crystals or Russian vine. There are questions in every proposition, but we pin down implications as best we can, weighted in each corner like a gingham cloth on a winter picnic, freezing in its billowing, emulating plump clouds and curved bellies. We listen to each other's voices layered through leaves, onion-sharp and tectonic, soughing in the ripple of metal and wires that bloom unaffordable trinkets. We are unconditionally receptive to each successive imbroglio, and even talk of silver screens can breed misunderstanding, so we speak with our palms, choose distraction over each discrete option, and salt words away against every conceivable dissolution.

Silvering the Mirror

There's a gull on the gate, a glass over the grate, a reflection of every face you've ever worn. There are names falling from the sky, seeding walls which sprout vaults and windows, each illuminated with familiar allegories and myths retold for a contemporary audience. In the aisles, meat undulates back into its animal persona: a transubstantiation of sorts; a transgressive metamorphosis that questions the integrity of bodies and intentions. Mirrors can't be held responsible for their visions, and sometimes lines of verse just don't know where to end, but we all remake ourselves to the shape of the same basic plots, whenever they return from the sea, whatever names claim.

What Is Wrong with this Picture?

Cameras catch what's left behind: a tear welling at the corner of a bloodshot eye; a window papered with last year's news; the patterns of frayed graffiti when the words have worn away. Dogs wait at doors for the missing and cats creep undisturbed amongst beached fish, tasting the elements that fill their waking dreams. There are clocks everywhere, the code of their captured semaphore the only framed detail that remains unbroken. I swallow hard, gagging on newsprint, feeling radiation flutter through my finest capillaries, and a small hand tugging at the hem of my borrowed coat. Light bleeds, fogging the negative, transitioning the tangible to ghosts. What's left behind is gelatin and silver halides fixed in sodium thiosulfate, the stink of vinegar, and unseen details beyond the visible spectrum.

Repeat to Fade

My internal monologue is an old talk stamped in wax, scratched into life by a rose thorn seeking a fresh vein, its words worn to nothing but guttural ululations: a pick of the pops for the Age of Oblivion; a siren song, submerged. A grey woman folds her grey clothes into a pagoda which may pass for silver when it catches the sunlight later on. When I blink she is gone but I will carry her breath on the base of my neck for days, maybe years. Muffled inflections hum me to sleep and tell me what I should dream: a scabbed path from needling rocks to a gleaming silver pagoda; a mermaid's scales weighing up the pros and cons of elemental exchange; a DJ scratching at the spinning world. Webbed fingers apply firm pressure to my bony hips, and warm wetness wreaths my waist. The words in my veins slough off sense layer by layer, until meaning is nothing but neatly folded clothes on the steps of a grey pagoda which is already forgetting the Silver Age. The runoff groove slurs its tongue-stunted grunting as a woman—who is she? should I recognise her?—folds her hands in her grey scaly lap.

THE BRONZE AGE

JEN WEBB

'Of Bronze — and Blaze —
The North — tonight —
So adequate —'
—*Emily Dickinson, '#319'*

'As bronze may be much beautified
By lying in the damp dark soil …'
—*Wilfred Owen, 'As Bronze'*

The quotations heading each section are from *Works and Days*, p41-42, in Hesiod 2006 *Theogony, Works and Days, and The Shield of Heracles* (transl Hugh Evelyn-White), New York, NY: Dover Publications.

Let the record show

He looks up from his crossword—'A five-letter word for
bronze dirt?' She looks up from brooding—'But doesn't
it just depend?' He nods, yes, and goes back to puzzle,
while she tries to connect the dots. There's no clear
answer, and if the holy tales ring true then anything can
be true. A man with fifty heads; men sprung from trees;
mad witches who wait to drink our blood. We, the middle
children of some taxonomy, play our bit parts in a reality
show. Meanwhile those bastards the gods toast us, their
obedient fools soon to turn to mud.

Parkour

You come down hard and remember to bounce, clever feet finding their level and every sprung muscle primed for a fall that will always turn to lift, as though someone prised the pins from a butterfly's wings and it tests the air on its line of flight. The man endlessly washing his hands looks up as you leap past his eyeline, hands reaching for the roof and finding its edge, and you swing up and over and away sweet chariot, and he opens the window, leans out to see nothing but a shadow on the sill, a trace of ash in the air.

Becoming tree

It was the weather they warned you to expect, rain then wind whimpering across the crown of the tree outside your door, the tree that groans on troubled nights; as do you. Find slippers and robe, take the scotch outside, pour a tot for the tree and another for you. You think the tree will tell how history finds its feet. It knows nothing; or less than you. Tree has watched the humans come and go, watched the weather change. It has nothing to say but *wait*.

Inheritance

When she left her lover she took only the spoon he had made her, with its plaited handle, all its hearts and its locks, a promise she had read as a debt. She forgot his name and the texture of his skin, but carried in a locked box the image of his knife and how it shone when he sat before the fire, whittling. Now she too has gone, walking down that path you picture but cannot parse. You hold the spoon tonight, as you have held it over the years, your hands translate its golden bowl to bronze. Now your thumb is full of splinters no one else can see, and you too are built of smoke and memories, a piece of cedar wood and a short-blade knife you whet on the worn-out stone, each pass across its surface doing double duty as regret.

Psych 101

Air like dry grass; light that absorbs the sound; she's
choking here, can't switch off attention, can't learn to
understand. *Understand what?* says the therapist, standing
beside the table where he keeps his calendar and the
photo of his favourite car, putting down his notepad and
reaching out his hand. She shakes her head, fumbling for
words that will fit in her mouth, words she can roll around
her tongue, can spit out onto the blotter on his desk and
she thinks she might arrange them into sense but stands,
instead, and leaves, very gently closing the door.

Storm

Wind whispers through the ash trees in the yard, rain whispers along the horizon and across the valley and dapples the pine deck, turning its blonde to bronze. It will not last beyond the hour; we watch the colour shift to steel, rain picks up its pace and shrubs begin to cringe beneath its blows. Later we will prune and weed, and gather the broken plants, and place them in the bin.

3. THEIR ARMOUR WAS OF BRONZE, AND THEIR HOUSES OF BRONZE, AND BRONZE WERE THEIR IMPLEMENTS ...

Plus ça change

You can count on this: that war is always on its way. The king writes to his allies, *Send me forces and chariots; save me*—but his staffer has already hit the road, and the letters are never sent. The staffer has locked away his records, and the king's; he has tucked his copy of the myths into his leather bag, shut the school his daughters ran, and together they have run. The Sea People are coming; the Age of Bronze is done. The merchant has one eye on the weather, the other on the world. With luck he might make it through.

Metamorphosis

The suburb is a maze of walls and shining gates. My house hides behind a fence of bronze and the sky reflects there, air becoming metal, cloud becoming stone. Where night meets day then blue turns to bronze, and the light becomes shimmer on my home, turning it hard-edged, and cold.

The colours of the season

They built gates of bronze; they shaped greaves of bronze, and spears. The world a shining jewel in autumn tones that would, I fancy, have flattered my skin, and I dress and step outside into sunset, the memory of bronze, the colour I have become, and I blend with the sky, vanish before my husband's eyes, becoming part of everything.

Museology

Inside the museum, hiding from these strange days,
strange sights, you gazing at the sarcophagus, at its bronze
sword, bronze pendant that must have pressed heavy across
a brazen heart. There's sword and shield and breastplate,
there's a man in greaves, a man in stripes, there's not
even a whiff of fear as they face invaders, knowing that
for them the end is emptiness. We are standing in a dark
display, with the cacophony of history outside the walls
but in here not even a ghost murmuring her tale. Inside
the dark, beyond the glass, the myth of golden men.

The forever war

Gunfire in the night, again, and the cats running home low to the ground. Fire against sky, the Great Bear scrambling to get its distance from us, and candles that soar high above the house where I am, chocolate on my tongue and pointing *there! there!* Mother wrapped a rug around me despite the heat, and took me back inside. Fed me chutney on store-bought bread. Fed me stories from forgotten northern lands. After she sang me to sleep, she set the alarms and sat that night, armed, before the door.

But nonetheless

It's September one which is to say—spring, as town will attest, its plum tree avenues all bold pink, ducklings peep from behind the tussocks, it's September one. Which is to say—precisely eighty-something years ago the war began which no one not even newsreaders will remember to attest. You cycle past crocodiles of children on their dragged-foot way to class, past schools of parrots who are working the grass, and on the surface of the lake float buildings and trees, the water shifts slightly, they sink. Frogs sing. Birds sing. Mostly we are new.

History

It comes with a whiff of the grave, a glimpse of bronze eagle in his armour, a pointless war. Bureaucrats draft policies that bear the memory of yesterday's disaster and the scars of past mistakes, and rulers read them, thoughtfully, attending to the arguments of advisors, reaching for their pens. Giving up is the price we pay for tomorrow; burning up, burning out, reaching for the fire hose.

Balancing the books

You are hunched over your ledger, calculator groaning quietly to itself, matching a with b or rather cost with benefit. Your wife, whom I choose not to consider, leaves a cup of coffee on your desk and closes the door. I have taken to prowling the streets, explaining to worried men I pass that I am seeking the perfect shot. It's not enough, is it? Your emails, my Insta posts, the connection we will never achieve. The reality you promised me is nothing but a veil. And when I googled your name yesterday the screen said *The page you are trying to view doesn't exist.* I knew this already.

Now your wife is dialling my number and hanging up when I respond. Your wife is doing your accounts and making secret plans. I have painted my walls with petrol but no matter where I look, I cannot find a flame.

Tree change

We wrestled with our records, trying to balance the books while documents disappeared from the screen and you hit the keys, knocking out a tune so tortured I had to leave. When you closed your eyes to reach the high notes I stole your ute, and your wallet, and waterbag, and was halfway to the coast before you reached high c. Now I am in the land of wild maps where kangaroos steal my coins and bronzewings lull me to sleep. I woke yesterday to find my arms full of scars, the sun gazing at me appalled, and the river creeping away. Now it's just me, and the alien birds, and hard days lying in wait, without a future to my name.

6. THEY LEFT NO NAME

Bronze Age hoard found intact in Essex field

Before we fled, before the raiders came, I dug a pit below the plough blade's reach. A grave for our goods, for the axe heads and bracelets and blades. Bury them, a clay box for a coffin. I shovel back the soil and leave them there, a record for those who will come in some unimaginable future to know we lived, despite the gods' decree; to know that we were more than the simple creatures of war.

Reading the archive

'the archive allows us to see clearly what formerly we could only glimpse'

My summer job at the Copper Kettle Café where every night I scrubbed the scent of fish from my hair, rubbed ash across my skin, but still I stank of grease. Early mornings in the sea; my back and legs turning bronze; and the farmers coming to collect their cakes would linger, eyes on my limbs, how I could move as though I had a hundred arms to summon up coffees and milkshakes without breaking stride, how I distributed doughnuts like sacrament. They loved me, they leaned across the high counter, leering but I loved you with your stories and the hut where you stored your box files and notes, where slowly you were building a card house of history, learning how to see.

Grave goods

You never stopped longing for the sight of the sea, for its scent. I sat beside you as you died, full of promises that I never forget. Tomorrow I will bring you the sea in a bottle—a handful of bronze sand poured through its mouth, a scoop of salt water with gesture of a wave, and tiny shells crimped across the lid. I will leave it on your grave, as you asked, showing I am still here and remember you; saying I still speak your name.

Surviving history

The cat beneath the canna lilies is waiting to draw blood.
I wear my heavy gloves, steel-capped shoes; you bear
scars on your calves but *That's nothing*, you say, describing
your grandfather's leopard scars, describing your uncle
who vanished into war. I balance on the edge of the cliff,
blindfolded, taking my chances with whatever comes
next, but you catch me up, determined we will stay in the
bright light of day.

New age

New ghosts drift uncertainly across the life they left, manifesting in family mirrors, hanging about the morgue aghast at the shape of themselves on the tray. It's the surprise that does for them, the unpreparedness. Books unburnt, letters never sent, no chance to tidy up. A day passes, and another and they watch how light dissolves into light, and the ferryman checks the time.

Being, not doing

There's something that smells like silk. There's an antique
sunset hung across the horizon. Behind you the famous
Bernini bronzes catch a final touch of light. Your mother
taught you how to see beauty in brokenness, the wealth
found in ditches and along the edge of paths, what is left
after the wasp has built its nest of mud, and flown away.

Notes

Section 1

The complete Hesiod (*Theogony, Works and Days, and The Shield of Heracles*), translated by Hugh Evelyn-White (New York: Dover Publications, 2006), presents a world where universes collide, or co-exist, violently. Three of the sons of Heaven and Earth had 'fifty heads' each, and a hundred arms (*Theogony*, p17). The people of the Bronze Age were confusingly 'sprung from ash-trees', though Proclus thinks that for 'ash-tree' read the nymphs called Meliae; and Goettling identifies the ash trees as the spears of the Bronze Age warriors (*Works and Days*, p41); in the battle between Perseus and the Gorgons, the Fates lurked around the edges, 'lowering, grim, bloody, and unapproachable, ... longing to drink dark blood' (*Shield of Heracles*, p63).

Section 3

Roger Atwood writes of a Late Bronze Age import/export merchant, Urtenu, whose surviving records—letters, business documents, extracts from the Epic of Gilgamesh—include desperate appeals for help in the face of drought, then famine, and then the invading Sea Peoples who eventually destroyed Ugarit.

Section 6

'Bronze Age hoard found intact in Essex field' is a headline from the BBC News, 31 October 2020.

The epigraph to 'Reading the archive' is taken from the archaeologist Yoram Cohen, cited in Roger Atwood (2021) 'The Ugarit archives', *Archaeology* 74.4 (July/August): 24–31, p27.

THE HEROIC AGE

CASSANDRA ATHERTON

'Through their heroic, harrowing, and heart-breaking accounts, we relive the tragic day that hastened the end of a war and changed the world forever.'

— *'The Day the Bomb Dropped'*, *WWII Special Collection*, 2015

'I mustn't let myself become the heroine of a tragedy. Even though I experienced the atomic bomb, I have many things in my life that I enjoy.'

— *Sachi Rummel*

Keiko Ogura

When Keiko Ogura invited me to step into the 'atomic space', I hesitated. I wasn't 2.4 km from the hypocentre. I wasn't alone on the north side of the road. I didn't see Hiroshima as a sea of fire. I am not hibakusha. This is not my story to tell. The 'nuclear sublime'; the 'atomic sublime'—these are euphemisms for the unnameable. I told Keiko I couldn't imagine it. She nodded and taught me to make a paper crane. I folded the paper, turning it over, but couldn't work out how to make the pocket. Keiko put her hands over my fingers and pressed down on the folds. She tugged open the paper pouch. I began to make the wings.

Hero Shima Diner

The head of a giant pussywillow fills half the diner. Its scarred trunk winds up through the floor, its branches pushing out through the roof as if a giant needle has stitched the diner into the sky. A man in a Carp baseball cap says, 'Hibakujumoku, survivor tree' and the chef gestures towards ten black and white photographs of women on the wall. 'A meal for a poem,' she says.

Hero Shima Diner: Okonomiyaki

I order okonomiyaki. Bonito flakes perform tai-chi atop layered noodles and fried egg, the paper-thin sheaves of fish waving and curling. One of the regulars asks me my name before writing it neatly in Japanese with a thick-nibbed fountain pen on a slip of paper. 'Bright,' she says pointing to one of her written characters. I point to another, 'cherry blossom—sakura,' I say. She smiles and nods. I cut along the lattice of mayonnaise and see the layers of cabbage and noodle suspended in the pancake matrix. It reminds me of a hot evening in Narita where I ordered cheesy teppanyaki noodles and you drank Asahi from a frosted stein. The chef places a box of okonomiyaki on the counter, Mutsumi-en Nursing Home written on the side in bright cherry blossom style. I take out my notebook and pen. 'For the lonely,' she says.

Photograph: Shigeko Niimoto

In one blinding flash, she is 'unmarriageable', with shiny
beetroot skin and gnarled paper palm hands. For a month
her mother smooths her skin with cooking oil before
peeling remnants of cloth and fragments of ash-coloured
flesh from her body. She is called 'Devil's Claw Marks',
'A-Bomb Maiden', and 'shame'. She suggests a twilight
society for disfigured women. The Reverend calls them
'Keloid Girls'. In America, her chin is fetishised in photos
as the stump of candle that has melted below the wick. A
dozen operations and skin grafts rebuild her face. Even
after she marries and bears a son, she is called 'Hiroshima
Maiden'.

Hero Shima Diner: Onsen Egg

The chef serves it in a flower shaped bowl, naked and bathing in dashi. I imagine it clothed in its shell, soaking in a hot spring. My onsen egg is half-boiled and in reverse—firm yolk and runny white. It's like a giant eyeball plucked from Cyclops' forehead. The gelatinous white is soft custard on my tongue and I remember the undercooked omelettes you ate at the breakfast buffet, bright orange yolk spotting your plate. At 8 p.m., one of the regulars takes a cuff and stethoscope out of her bag. 'Some won't go to the doctor, so Hina created Nurses Station Night,' the chef tells me. I squeeze the yolk with my chopsticks and wonder how many patrons she has saved. The yellow sphere is shiny, like a lacquered sun.

Photograph: Sadako Kurihara

She was four kilometres north of the epicentre. She writes
about it, but censorship destroys her lines with thick black
boxes and overscoring. Her notebooks from high school
are filled with haiku; now new poems rupture traditional
forms. The blank page is ground zero. She sees beyond
its edges and past Hiroshima. Her testimony burns. She
is midwife at the birth of the atomic bomb. Her pen is
heavy. In free verse, she reminds us all—we are sitting on
black eggs.

Hero Shima Diner: Kaki Furai

Plump with frilled edges, the chef plucks them from their pointed shells. The adductor muscles are transparent, like portholes. She hands me a shell and, as I drink from the hinge, the oyster liquor is a delicate spill of the sea. They call the fisherwoman Ryuji, because she saved her brother from drowning. She has supplied these oysters for thirty years and, deep fried, they are robed in golden breadcrumbs. There is silence apart from the crunching in my ears. I tell the chef I will write a second poem for a glass of plum wine. I plunge my tongue into the sticky amber liquid. Brine and sweetness mix on my tastebuds. I wonder if I could be an oyster harvester, have an oyster farm, be your Hiroshima pearl.

Photograph: Tetsuko Shakuda

Hiroshima's resurrection begins hours after it is mostly obliterated. While the ashes are still hot, she gets the tram moving again. Injured people stare through open windows at the city's seething remains. The city is buried under bodies and wreckage. She is only fourteen, she has an upset stomach and feels weirdly light-headed. There is a wide silence, apart from the tram clattering along the realigned tracks. She is still haunted by the swarms of flies, imagines them feasting on distended bodies clinging to the tram's roof. The city is burning junkyard and desert but the tram's bell rings.

Photograph: Midori Naka

In the soft morning light, she makes tea for the Sakura-tai troupe. The curve of the teapot's handle presses on her palm as she recites her lines: 'Life is no more than the repeated fulfilling of a permanent desire.' The small white cups are crackle glazed, their hairlines like silver scars. Waking naked under rubble, she remembers a blast, as if a hot water boiler exploded. Silence. Under the stripe of bright light, her white blood cells deplete. Leaving behind the smouldering charcoal of Hiroshima, she returns by train to Tokyo. Days later, her remains are floating in two glass jars. Wet archive, the wrinkled and brown tissue looks like decomposing plums. I think of cherry blossom petals bruised underfoot or the unripe fruit in bottles of plum wine.

Hero Shima Diner: Yaki Gyoza

Five crescent moons on a black rectangular plate, the gyoza nestle against one another, curve inside curve. As I eat, I remember the winged gyoza you ate in Narita and how we laughed when you said they were surrealist dumplings. I nudge the end of one into the tangy dipping sauce and chilli sticks to its skin—like a raised, spicy rash. The chef packs a bag with leftover scraps of cooked meat, fish and steamed vegetable offcuts. 'Soft food for the Seniors Sanctuary,' she says and from the window I see three young women in pink t-shirts walking eleven elderly dogs. The woman next to me asks if someone will feed me soft food and walk me when I get old. As I eat my final gyoza, I save its crispy belly for last, imagining it with wings.

Photograph: Michiko Osawa

The house is slowly crushing the three of them to death, pressing air from their chests and sound from their lips. Trapped for seventeen hours, her sister whimpers because the baby is no longer moving in her belly. When a foreigner digs them out, slices of skin have been torn from her mother's forehead, right arm and knees, exposing bone. Two days later, her sister delivers a stillborn child with chubby limbs and thick black hair. She swaddles it in tears, laying it on her bruised chest as if her ragged breath might resurrect it. An army surgeon operates on them without anaesthetic, hollowing out rotting flesh like the black flesh of a decomposing banana. When her other sisters arrive from Tochigi prefecture and Yokohama, they do not recognise her.

Hero Shima Diner: Takoyaki

Lightly pricking the dashi batter, the chef spins the takoyaki balls in their honeycombed pan. Golden all over, gooey inside, I squeeze a sphere against the roof of my mouth, searching for the diced octopus in the centre. Once we ordered takoyaki at Koko and you turned over my half-eaten spheres so they looked whole again. One of the regulars hands me a flyer. She's directing the Peace Boat—hibakusha will tell their stories to passengers as it sails between Hiroshima and Nagasaki. I look at my plate. The atomic bomb's core was the size of a takoyaki ball, but six thousand times as hot as the sun.

Photograph: Hatsuyo Nakamura

She washes the rice until cloudy water runs clear. While she reads the Hiroshima *Chugoku*, the grains bloat as they soak—the fatter they become, the fluffier the rice will be. There are more Japanese words for *rice* than *love*, but what she feels for her children won't be spoken. As the rice cooks, she turns it from the bottom. The children are still on their bedrolls, tired from the air raids. She hands them some peanuts and prepares for piecework on her husband's Sankoku sewing machine. She sees the seven words from the telegram in the bubbles bursting through the water in the boiling pot: 'Isawa died an honorable death at Singapore.' White flash in the window. They are buried. She crawls out from under tiles and broken beams, following the small voices to their entombment. As she digs them out from under the wreckage, her five-year-old asks, 'Why is it already night?' 'Why did our house fall down?' In the Spring, she clears a space to plant a vegetable garden, they eat off plates scavenged from the debris. The sewing machine rusts in the water tank.

Hero Shima Diner: Saba Sashimi

Spangled skin sitting atop a triangle of vivid cerise and translucent flesh, the saba is served on a wooden board with a Shiso leaf and pea sprouts, like long-stemmed flowers. One of the patrons smiles as I balance a piece of the mackerel on my chopsticks. I recognise her as the feminist activist who sparked the 'Flower Demo' to protest sexual violence. I remember pressing a white blossom into my journal as we walked back to our hotel after eating our first saba sashimi. We followed the chef's advice, eschewing soy sauce and wasabi for the mackerel's creamy texture.

Photograph: Setsuko Thurlow

A code breaker in school uniform, she looks for patterns and symbols in American military reports. She has cracked several cryptic notes but as she crawls toward light and a soldier's voice, she cannot decipher what has happened. Reborn in charcoal, she is a smudge on the broken landscape. Bodies cross the city. As she steps over and around them, dying people beg in whispers, 'water, please, water', hands reaching for her ankles. She takes off her shirt and soaks it in the river. Touching the wet fabric to their blistered lips, they begin to suckle. They die quickly, to be resurrected in the bluish light of her anti-nuclear narratives. When she wins the Nobel Peace Prize, the Japanese Prime Minister turns his back on her achievements.

Hero Shima Diner: Scallop Nigiri and Sashimi

Huge snowy pillows spot the plate, their tops are mirror glazed.
The chef butterflies each one, wrapping tiny sashes around the
place where they are joined. 'Scallops two ways,' she says, 'two
more poems.' She takes a blow torch and caramelises the shiny
faces of half the scallops—a mixture of sashimi and aburi style
on a deep blue mukozuke. One of the regulars starts sewing the
hem on a small pink hat with yellow butterflies and long ties.
When she catches me watching she says, 'chemotherapy bonnets'
and I think about the time we watched a chef create small pods
of seasoned rice with one hand. Now I imagine them shaped
like the atomic bomb memorial. He draped the spliced scallops
over the rice mounds. We ate in silence.

Photograph: Sadako Sasaki

Her story is governed by numbers. It is a decade since the atomic bomb was dropped and she is the fastest runner in the ragged class, sprinting fifty metres in seven and a half seconds. In hospital, doctors measure her fluctuating temperature and white blood cell count. She believes if she folds a thousand paper cranes she will recover. In bed, she makes over sixteen hundred from scrap paper, and her brother keeps one tiny crane she folded with a pin from a candy wrapper. In her casket she lies on a bed of one thousand paper cranes. Now, one hundred-and-twenty more sit in the Hiroshima Memorial Peace Museum; one is displayed at Pearl Harbor. Each year, ten million paper cranes are sent to the Children's Peace Monument from around the world. Her brother remembers taking her to the rooftop to see the stars. There were far too many to count.

Photograph: Mitsuno Ochi

The shape of a woman with a walking stick is scorched onto
the stairs at the entrance of the Sumimoto bank. Waiting
for the bank to open, she absorbed the boiling light,
blocking heat from the stone. Nuclear daguerreotype,
her shadow is stone-blasted and, like an old crime scene,
the body is outlined in chalk. Everything around her is
bleached. Someone claims the shadow as her mother.
Precious relic, she is every woman who disappeared.

Hero Shima Diner: Hay Smoked Bonito

Sweet smoke rises as the huge bonito is gently smoked over nests of hay. When it's ready, the chef demonstrates how to place the smooth slice of garlic, long curve of white onion and small bundle of cabbage on the triangle of magenta flesh. A form of ikebana, four of us create sprays of vegetables atop our bright slices of fish. In one large bite, my mouth presses the crisp onion into the smoky flesh. I order a Highball, remembering the time we said 'omakase' and the chef torched the skin of a red snapper. We heard the sizzle and watched it curl at the edges in orange sparks. One of the regulars, Miho, asks the chef if she will pin up a flyer. It's a free class for young people on nuclear policy and TPNW. I ask her about the acronym and she explains, Treaty on the Prohibition of Nuclear Weapons. I hand my poems to the chef and when I'm halfway down the narrow staircase I hear Miho say, 'Tread carefully, there are bones beneath our feet.'

Photograph: Emiko Okada

In the bloodied sky, she sees Hiroshima burning. As sunset cloaks buildings in crimson, their windows are the yellow eyes of victims. She hides in shadows and prays to the wind to change direction. The backs of her legs are red-hot but now she cannot stop running. Flash sickness confirms her exposure. She has no burns or keloids but her gums start bleeding and her hair comes away in handfuls. Decades later, she shows students the relics, tells them when the sun is scarlet in the northwest, she hears her sister say, 'I will see you later'. She never returns.

Hero Shima Diner

*It's late. A triptych of buttercup fabric floats above a narrow
staircase. My backpack is heavy, my gold jacquard dress sticks to
my skin. I've walked the city—its grids, bridges, waterways—
but I'm not ready to catch the tram back to the station. Standing
in front of the cenotaph, it felt like the soil vibrated under my
feet—but the sky was a stilly blue. As I climb the stairs one last
time, there are no more poems to write. I think of you sending
me photos from your balcony of the fireworks, the explosions of
rupturing light.*

THE IRON AGE

PAUL MUNDEN

'Show me someone with no ego and I'll show you a big loser'

—Donald Trump

'It Was Good While It Lasted'

—Jimmy Savile

21 SELFIES

#1 with BoJo

When Boris visited the bacon factory where I worked, I thought this is the future, chumming up with blokes like him, not those morons in the Baco. Slaving away in a crap job, what's the point? I like his hair, and it was cruel to make him wear that plastic net. Jimmy Savile, he had that same nice superblonde look. I thought of fotoshopping Farage in, but he's a poxy little pillock, his hay day has gone. Also, it's sort of cheating. As a kid, I never once made it onto *Jim'll Fix It*, and that hurt. He was a hero to kids like me. But I managed to get a secondhand badge off ebay, all in red capitals: JIM FIXED IT FOR ME. Never looked back. He had a bad press, no chance to defend himself, so nothing was really proved. But buried in a gold coffin, what's not to like!

#2 on a rollercoaster

Sometimes the readymade thrills don't cut it. Once you've done your first vertical loop they're all much the same. One trick is to think of the times when they've crashed, but that's almost as unlikely as winning the lottery, not that I'm totally oh fay with the stats. What you don't see here is how I threw up, tilting my head so that the chunky yellow vomit flew back over the kids behind me in the open cars. I bet that really made their day!

#3 on a level crossing

I decided to take things up a notch, sitting in my car, across the rails, both hands off the wheel. The challenge was to keep looking straight ahead, not to either side, as that would risk catching an early sight of the oncoming train. Just wait to hear it getting close. I had the earpods in, playing Motorhead, but reckoned I would pick up the rumble through the rails. It's funny the things that go through your head in that situation. Trains you've missed, trains that never arrived, people tied to the track as some corny setup for a film, or waking from some horrible dream where you're the victim!

#4 with the Mona Lisa

Bloody difficult, I can tell you, getting my own smile to line up. And it's a halfarsed smile in the first place, isn't it? The crowds are something else. I know you can't really see much of the art, but you can get that on the Louver site. Call me shallow, but there are loads of deeply shallow people earning big bucks in these galleries. I've made quite a study. A urinal, a stuffed shark, a pile of bricks, people using their own excrement on a canvas. Why would anyone pay good money for that? Just how stupid do they think we are?!

#5 with a lump of coal

This is a whole stack of selfies in one, my tribute to the entire Australian government. Postmodern or whatever they call it. But Jeezus what a bunch of ugly mugs. Who'd want to be seen dead with them in person? The idea is pretty sound though. Who's afraid of a piece of dirt? Maybe those tossers with their solar powered cars and windfarmed chickens. As Scomo says, 'Wind doesn't always blow, sun doesn't always shine'. I like it when people tell it like it is. Also when Tony Abbott, the guy with the budgie smugglers, gave Prince Philip a knighthood. Comedy gold!

#6 with a forest fire

You can really feel the heat in this one. I was risking life and limb, though what use is a limb if you've lost your life? That sort of thing gives me sleepless nights. I once tried starting a fire myself, but I used so much petrol my fucking fingers were burnt and I dropped the phone. It was an iPhone X, too. But wouldn't you know it, some insurance I didn't even know I had gave me a new one. New model. Result!

#7 with Bolsonaro

I love how the guys behind us, the loggers, are holding their chainsaws like guitars. Or you know what. Nice brown backdrop. Perfect album cover for a heavy metal band. Felt like I was mingling with the gods. The worst thing I ever saw was Clint Eastwood singing 'I talk to the trees'. What a disgrace after Dirty Harry, should have been banned. Expensive trip, this, but what's a bucket list for? As Lemmy says, 'that's the way I like it baby, I don't wanna live for ever'!
[show more]

#8 with a dead rhino

A magnificent beast, am I not? The animal's hide is rather rubbish, like drying mud. You have to be tough as nails for this sort of thing, and pay through the nose. Also, afterwards, really really thick skinned, given the abuse you get on social media. But I'd say it's worth it. You can even make a further killing with the powdered horn!

#9 taking the knee

Respect to my mate Tommy for blacking up. We made a class double act. Tommy said it felt quite nice, and I'd have to agree. Cushion like, comfy all round. Looks a bit daft to me all those footballers doing it with no kneelers, just grass. Like sinkronised swimmers come to a halt. Artistic swimming they're calling it now, ffs. People get really hot under the collar about sport and politics, let alone so called art muscling in, and I don't blame them. A medal round your neck is what matters. No one wants you spoiling the national anthem. I'm shocked though to read they're not the actual metals. Can you believe it? And what's that thing with biting them like chocolate money wrapped in foil? Back in the day, they gave the real thing at primary school sports day. I've got a genuine bit of silver for coming second in the sack race. Nowadays I'd get gold, different kind of sack!

#10 with a magnum of Dom Perignon

On the podium, where I belong. And not with any old bottle, this one was priced at over 42 grand. See the label? What did I win I can hear you asking, but that's not really the point. More importantly, not a drop of this was drunk, how sick is that? Posh wine turned into a gush of pure, pointless froth. A connorsewer, that's me!

#11 with some statue

I don't even know who this guy is, but I'm told he made a packet. Something to do with sugar, wtf? This was just before all the wokies went on the rampage. Cunts. I've had nicer times with Millwall supporters. There was a bit of a scuffle, but the police did well, and we had a pretty wild time afterwards, in the Colston Arms. 15 pints of Vanguard lager, and still standing!

#12 at Ground Zero

You had to be quick. What's the point in being one of the five million a year who visit it once it's all cleared up and turned into a museum? I was a bit put out when Trump got there first, but laughed when he talked about 7-Eleven. As it happens, I've seen the museum too, and it's not all that bad. It's over the site with the actual remains. There's video simulation of the attacks, real phone calls from people on the planes. Mangled metal from the towers. Footage of people jumping to their deaths, though I'd seen all that on TV. There's one windowpane that survived intact, which did my head in. The history stuff gets boring though. I mean, who wants to know about the middle east? There's quite a good gift shop. I bagged some jewellery and a FDNY teddy for my niece. Everyone's confused that the attacks were in September, not November, not surprising really, since Americans put the date the wrong way round!

#13 with Jimmy Savile

This post has been removed

#14 with my neighbour

She has cancer, so I think I'm being brave here. People I
trust say cancer is catching, dogs can even smell it. Her
hair doesn't look very good, does it, though you never
know, that could be a scam, to get sympathy and cash.
I'm in awe of that girl who faked having cancer then
claimed to have cured it with some lunatic diet. A million
instagram followers, just like that, all buying the app.
Influencer, now there's a good job, AND a good word,
makes me think of influenza!

#15 dressed as you know who

This was for a party, and yeah, I worry that it isn't totally original. I saw the Shy Prince get publicity for something similar. I'm in the white version, which he wore through the summer. Double breasted, with matching white trousers. Not the sort of thing to shit yourself in. Matching white visor cap. I'm told the swastika is an old religious symbol of good luck, but it clearly didn't work for him!

#16 wearing Kanye West's trainers

I did a whole sequence of this sort of thing. It's surprising how cheap you can find stuff worn by the stars, online. Not all of them are seriously famous, I'll give you that. So when these came up, I thought bingo, el dorado. His music is crap, and he was probably right to piss on his own Grammy. Still, fame is fame. I knew I'd need to go the whole nine yards, and was hanging on in, but when the bidding went over six million, I had to pull out. That wasn't the end of the story though. The guy who won was a real sport, and let me take this photo pretending they're mine!

#17 without a mask

In the thick of it. Sometimes a crowd is just what you need, for maximum effect, cough cough cough. I did have one in my pocket, as I wasn't going to be arrested. Not my style, no slurree. I sometimes put it on, but hanging loose, under my nose, sometimes mouth. People seem to get angrier at that than if you're not wearing one at all. People have the craziest phobias, that's for sure. Anyway, I like to think I've done my bit for herd immunity against the coroner thingy, and led the way back to normalsea. Love the sound of that. Can't find it in the dictionary, which makes me well chuffed. Ahead of the game yet again! #sheeple

#18 as a stalker

See that girl in front of me, in the blue-buttoned dress?
She could hear me muttering and started to walk faster.
I set myself the task of following her home, and made it
all the way, no one batting an eyelid. That was enough for
one day. It's harder to know the next step. Also to think
of a decent name. Yorkshire Ripper, Suffolk Strangler,
they've all been nabbed, so maybe I should use this post as
research, hoping people will come up with ideas!
[show less]

#19 *with a refugee*

There you go, I can do compassion just fine. I feel she could have smiled, having made it here from some shithole country with a life of freeloading ahead of her. People risked their lives to get her off the boat, which of course was a dumb thing to do. I refriended Farage when he said how the RNLI was a taxi service for illegal immigrants. Spot on. Brexit was supposed to have stopped all this, the reason I voted. The Remoaners call it ironic, but I don't really understand that, to be honest. After this shot I tripped her up and she fell flat on her face in a puddle!

#20 *with the Justified Ancients of Mu-Mu*

Aka The JAMs. Aka The KLF. Aka The K Foundation. Aka K2 Plant Hire Ltd, there's maybe more. To me they were just Jimmy and Bill, true geezers. At the BRITs, some classical conductor said he'd never heard anything as loud. Where had he been all his miserable life? I bet he missed their finest hour, burning a million quid of their hard earned cash when the Tate turned them down. The way they tell it, it was a bit of a fiasco, took well over an hour to burn, with some of the 50s just flying up the chimney. Their mate Gimpo filmed it all on Super 8. It's nice to see a band that doesn't give up or fade away, but keeps reinventing itself. Best of all was them giving out a vanload of super strength lager to the losers sleeping rough at Waterloo. That's charity at its finest. As Jimmy said, 'If you are down-and-out, would you rather have a bowl of soup or a can of Tennent's?' I lost the plot a bit at their Welcome To The Dark Ages event. The Toxteth Day Of The Dead sounded like fun, but it turned out they were planning a 'People's Pyramid', each brick made from someone's ashes. Creepy. But as the boys sang, 'K Cera Cera'!

#21 with self

I bet you were guessing this would be my own dick. Ok,
I had planned it, but the site rules have changed and it
wouldn't upload. Instead, you've got to look quite closely,
I'm the kid in the old chocolate bar ad on the TV behind
me. My mum recorded it all those years ago. Not sure
what prompted me to dig it out. But I vaguely remember
the hours hanging around in a backstage room. Someone
running his hand through my hair. My mum seemed a bit
upset by it all, and they didn't even give us much chocolate
to go away with. As soon as I took this I felt rather sick,
turned it off, and threw away the tape. Got rid of the
video nasties on the shelf, and took the player to the skip.
On my way home I thought I may have had enough of this
whole selfie thing.

Notes

#7   Clint Eastwood sang the song referenced in *Paint Your Wagon* (1969). *Dirty Harry* was filmed later, 1971.

#20   The classical conductor referenced is Sir Georg Solti. He won a BRIT award in 1992 for his recording of *Otello*, with Pavarotti, at a ceremony opened by the KLF in collaboration with Extreme Noise Terror. Their performance ended with Bill Drummond firing a machine gun (albeit with blanks) at the audience; their original concept had been even more disturbing. Accepting his award (presented by Right Said Fred) Solti commented: 'I must tell you a confession, I always thought that my daughter['s] bedroom was the noisiest place ... but after tonight['s] noise, I must make an apology'. The show was produced by Jonathan King, later convicted of child sexual abuse.

https://www.youtube.com/watch?v=pj5n2goJrz4&list=RDpj5n2goJrz4&index=1

INDIVIDUAL POET STATEMENTS

Paul Hetherington

THE GOLDEN AGE

The golden age is a beguiling concept that, in the extant literature, first makes its appearance in Hesiod's works. However, given the ubiquity and power of the idea, Hesiod would not have originated the concept—and, indeed, religious and cultural traditions and stories in much of Europe, Asia and the Middle East refer to some form of a golden age. For Hesiod, this age was when people 'lived as if they were gods,/ their hearts free from all sorrow,/ by themselves, and without hard work or pain' (1965: 31). This is an Edenic vision before the biblical Fall—or, as the pre-Christian Hesiod says, it was 'the beginnings of things,/ which were the same for gods as for mortals' (31).

After 'the earth has gathered over this generation', as Hesiod writes, the idea of gold is often much more literal. It is associated with earthly riches, status and power as well as with what is good and benign. Even as early as Plato's famous *Dialogues*, composed between about 400 and 347 BCE, various literal, symbolic and metaphorical significances of gold are frequently mentioned, including Hesiod's ideas. Even earlier, Homer often refers to the importance of gold in both the *Iliad* and *Odyssey*. The archaic, classical and Hellenistic Greeks mined gold extensively, as did the ancient Romans. Many civilisations that predated them had done the same and, in one demonstration of this, between 1972 and 1991 a 6,500-year-old gold hoard was excavated in Bulgaria, 'created only a few centuries after the first migrant farmers moved into Europe' (Curry 2016: n.p.). Among other artefacts, it contains 'pendants and bracelets, flat breastplates and tiny beads, stylized bulls and a sleek headpiece' (2016: n.p.). Gold has extraordinary properties, as well as wide appeal, being highly stable and generally resistant to acids. Modern science has established its astonishing malleability that allows it to be drawn out into a monoatomic wire.

The 21 prose poems on the golden age probe many of the connections I have mentioned and explore some of the contradictions between the purer or nobler associations of gold in various cultures and literatures and its (usually) simultaneous links with material wealth, greed, warfare, bloodshed and art. Gold has been the subject of many literary works and countless folk stories. It has been used to make or adorn many works in the visual and plastic arts traditions. It has come to stand in for the idea of what is untarnished and defies time. It has been tied to wisdom and justice, and also to class divisions. The *Bible* connects it to religious belief and devotion, and also to sacrilege and idolatory. It has, indeed, become such a complex and multidimensional metaphor and symbol that a group of prose poems can barely begin to address the complications, complexities and contradictions of gold's various denotations and connotations. However, it has been enjoyable to make a start and I hope readers will find at least one or two golden notions in these works.

Works Cited

Curry, Andrew 2016 'Mystery of the Varna Gold: What Caused these Ancient Societies to Disappear?', *Smithsonian Magazine*, 18 April: https://www.smithsonianmag.com/travel/varna-bulgaria-gold-graves-social-hierarchy-prehistoric-archaelogy-smithsonian-journeys-travel-quarterly-180958733/

Hesiod 1965 *The Works and Days, Theogony, the Shield of Herakles* (transl Richmond Lattimore), Ann Arbor, MI: The University of Michigan Press

Oz Hardwick

THE SILVER AGE (ENDLESSLY REFRACTED)[1]

Now we see ourselves, now we don't.

As far back as the eighth or ninth century BCE, Hesiod wrote of a child 'raised by his doting mother for one hundred years—a complete/ fool, gamboling in his own house,'[2] and the border—if border there is—between fidelity and foolhardiness remains as problematic as—if not more problematic than—it ever was.[3] Fools may be born with silver spoons in their mouths,[4] silver-tongued devils have the sharpest words, and just because there is no pre-Roman evidence, there is no earthly reason why the long spoon with which one should sup with the devil should not be silver.[5] Thirty pieces of silver can buy betrayal,[6] but Cornelia Parker's 1988-89 work of the same name, while explicitly making reference 'to money, to betrayal, to death and resurrection,' is, more significantly, 'about materiality and then about anti-matter': as Parker notes, 'the pieces of silver have much more potential when their meaning as everyday objects has been eroded.'[7]

Ultimately, as André Breton observed, 'historical anecdotes are not enormously important,'[8] but on Thursday 13 July 1972, Hawkwind appeared on the BBC's long-running music programme *Top of the Pops* with 'Silver Machine', their second single release, accompanied by an impressionistic collage of live footage from a recent performance at Dunstable Civic Hall.[9] Prompted by Alfred Jarry's essay, 'How to Construct a Time Machine', Robert Calvert's lyrics, while simultaneously suggesting both space travel and psychedelic drug experience, were in fact about a silver bicycle—or perhaps a perfect, archetypal silver bicycle which exists in one form or another at all times when one calls it to mind.[10]

Both 'Thirty Pieces of Silver' and 'Silver Machine' are preserved on YouTube,[11] though ultimately all moving images will dissolve, leaving only a film-thin silver border.[12] This is normal.[13] Inevitably, the shape that we recognise as the word 'silver'—and the word, as Hugo Ball asserted, 'is a public concern of the first importance'—will render itself nothing but afterimage and clouds.[14] Consequently, it is advisable for the century-old child to cycle home and keep a close eye on the weather.

> I did not err: there does a sable cloud
> Turn forth her silver lining on the night
> And casts a gleam over this tufted grove.[15]

The irrefutable laws of physics assure us there's time to change,[16] but there are no prizes for second best, other than a silver medal.

'One man praises one day; another praises another; but few really know.'[17]

Notes

1 The Filmetrics Refractive Index Database cites the refractive index and extinction coefficient at 632.8 nm for a typical sample of silver as 0.13511 and 3.985137: https://www.filmetrics.com/refractive-index-database/Ag/Silver. They do, however, add the caveat: 'No guarantee of accuracy—use at your own risk'. Neither they nor I can be held responsible for problems which may arise from overconfidence in employing these figures.

2 Hesiod, *Works and Days*, in *The Poems of Hesiod* 2017 (transl Barry Powell), Oakland, CA: University of California Press, ll. 114-5.

3 A pilgrim's garb from 1571, reproduced in Roob, Alexander 2014 *The Hermetic Museum: Alchemy and Mysticism*, Los Angeles, CA: Taschen, 564, brings to mind Hugo Ball's famous costume in which he performed his sound poem *Karawane* at the Cabaret Voltaire in 1916. There is something important here, if we can only pin it down.

4 The Sutton Trust and Social Mobility Commission report, *Elitist Britain 2019*, concluded that 'Britain's most influential people are over 5 times more likely to have been to a fee-paying school than the general population': https://www.gov.uk/government/news/elitism-in-britain-2019.

5 For the earliest known reference to this popular proverb, see *The Squire's Tale* in Chaucer, Geoffrey 1988 *The Riverside Chaucer* (ed Larry D Benson), Oxford: Oxford University Press, v (f) 602. The proverbial scene is vividly depicted on a late fifteenth-century misericord in St George's Chapel, Windsor—a wise maxim for monarchs. For an illustration, see James, MR 1933 *St George's Chapel, Windsor: The Woodwork of the Choir*, Windsor, 55.

6 Matthew: 26: 15.

7 *British Art Show* 1990 exhibition catalogue, London: Hayward Gallery, 88, quoted at https://www.tate.org.uk/art/artworks/parker-thirty-pieces-of-silver-t07461.

8 Tristan Tzara et al., *Twenty-Three Manifestos of the Dada Movement (1920)*, in Danchev, Alex (ed) 2011 *100 Artists' Manifestos from the Futurists to the Stuckists*, London: Penguin, 166-88 (182).

9 On the single, the performance, and the impact of the record's success on the band's fortunes—it rose to no. 3 on the official chart— see Banks, Joe 2020 *Hawkwind: Days of the Underground. Radical Escapism in the Age of Paranoia*, London: Strange Attractor, 78-96. On the broadcast's immeasurable impact on my twelve-year-old self, see Hardwick, Oz 2014 'It Started with a Disc,' *R2/Rock'n'Reel* 2.44, 130. The whole shared experience back then, of seeing such a performance, then enthusing about it with friends in the school playground the following day, feels now like a different world, a lost Golden Age. In Hesiod's words, we 'lived like gods, without/ a care in [our] hearts, far away from pain and suffering' (Hesiod, *Works and Days* (as above), ll. 100-1). By the time I became a regular in the early 1980s, the venue was known as Dunstable Queensway Hall.

10 '"Silver Machine" was just to say, I've gotta silver bicycle … I did actually have a silver racing bike when I was a boy. I've got one now, in fact.' Calvert, Robert 1981 Interview in *Cheesecake* 5, 6-11 (8). What distinguishes one of these bicycles from the other, except for time?

11 I saw 'Thirty Pieces of Silver' in the deconsecrated church of St Mary in York (UK), within easy walking distance of my house: the installation may be seen at https://www.youtube.com/watch?v=KlUefdrGhVs. Probably the best quality upload of that seminal broadcast of 'Silver Machine' is: https://www.youtube.com/watch?v=lrQICD4lZ4Y.

12 Film, from OE, *fell* = skin.

13 'Normal,' for the purposes of this discussion, may be defined as the ability to 'perform contrary actions together while taking one fresh gulp of air': Tristan Tzara, *Dada Manifesto (1918)*, in *100 Artists' Manifestos* (as above), 136-44 (137).

14 Hugo Ball, *Dada Manifesto (1916)*, in *100 Artists' Manifestos* (as above), 126-9 (129).

15 Milton, *Comus*, ll. 223-5.

16 Oz Hardwick, 'The Silver Age', in this very book, p. 27–51. Refraction and reflection: repetition, repetition, repetition.

17 Hesiod, *Works and Days* (as above), ll. 694-5. This is how my poems were composed.

Jen Webb

THE BRONZE AGE: CONTRA HESIOD

Hesiod's account of the Bronze Age is as hard—and hard-hearted—as the metal itself. He characterises its people as 'terrible and strong', warlike and violent, the losers in the taxonomy of time, who leave no mark on the earth, whose names are forgotten. Ovid has almost nothing to say about the Bronze Age, only that it was a time 'when cruel people were inclined to arms but not to impious crimes'. Their piety did them no service; they were shut away out of sight and mind by the gods they did not offend. I take issue with both Hesiod and Ovid, and their narrow perspectives, not least because the peoples of this age contributed so much more than war. It is a time of technological development, of migration and of trade. It is the birth of writing, with surviving records of business dealing, personal and official records, narratives including the *Epic of Gilgamesh*; and of course, a time of poetry. A Ugarit poem, 'Ritual of National Unity', conveys a picture of a community who for at least a while showed genuine interest in the rights and wellbeing of groups normally marginalised—women; foreigners (Pardee 2002; Boyes 2021). Which brings me to my second argument with these scholars of the ancient world (or their translators): the term 'Ages of Man' does not include women; and women at various points during the Bronze Age world had real autonomy. They could write; they could conduct business; they could rule a nation in their own right (Thomas 2014). This was, after all, the birth of modernity. And, contra Hesiod, who buries the Bronze Age in the backrooms of Hades, deleting them from the world of life and all its records, its people have left a substantial corpus of materials, texts, knowledge and, in some cases, even their names.

Works Cited

Pardee, Dennis 2002 *Ritual and Cult at Ugarit*, Atlanta, GA: Society of Biblical Literature

Boyes, Philip J 2021 *The Social Context of Writing Practices in Late Bronze Age Ugarit*, Oxford & Philadelphia: Oxbow Books

Thomas, Christine Neal 2014 *Reconceiving the House of the Father: Royal Women at Ugarit*, doctoral dissertation, Harvard University

Cassandra Atherton

In January 2021, the Science and Security Board moved the Doomsday Clock forward to 100 seconds to midnight, stating:

> the pandemic serves as a historic wake-up call, a vivid illustration that national governments and international organizations are unprepared to manage nuclear weapons and climate change, which currently pose existential threats to humanity, or the other dangers— including more virulent pandemics and next-generation warfare—that could threaten civilization in the near future.' (Mecklin 2021: n.p.)

Annihilation of the human race is, once again, on many people's minds.

This sequence of poems is a response to the need to understand why the atomic bomb was dropped on Hiroshima and its lasting effect on the city and its people. In 2015, I attended the ceremony for the 70th anniversary of the bombing. The mayor of Hiroshima, Kazumi Matsui, called for an end to nuclear weapons and, while the Japanese Prime Minister, Shinzo Abe, agreed, he simultaneously sought to renounce the pacifist Article 9 of the Constitution and re-arm Japan. More recently, President Obama hesitated before committing to visiting Hiroshima for fear of offending an American public that overwhelmingly believes that dropping the bomb was justified. Highlighting the complexity, Whitehouse spokesperson Josh Earnest promised that there would be no Presidential apology for the bomb, whilst also criticising North Korea for developing nuclear weapons. All of this, however, simply highlights the ongoing relevance of Hiroshima and the need to continue to seek deeper understandings of the bomb's significance and creative answers to related questions concerning humanity and its possible extinction.

Keiko Ogura, who survived the atomic bombing, told me that in lobbying for a nuclear free world, 'Imagination is key'. She believes writers, artists and poets are able to encourage empathy in their readers and are the way forward. However, this 'way forward' can be exacting and my biggest challenge in writing my prose poems was ensuring that I didn't appropriate the experiences the works refer to—I lay no claim to trying to understand what it must have been like to live through or witness the bombing. I also thought it important that this sequence of prose poems was not entirely abject and overwhelming. The film and screenplay *Hiroshima Mon Amour* became a key text for me because, while acknowledging the horror of what took place in the city, Marguerite Duras is nevertheless able to create a finely drawn love affair between a French woman and a Japanese man.

Academic and mythologist Joseph Campbell defines a hero as 'someone who has given his or her life to something bigger than oneself' (1998: 123). In this sequence of prose poems, I wanted to respond to both Hesiod's conception of the Heroic Age and Campbell's definition by composing a sequence that emphasised the importance of women in the atomic and post-atomic landscape. In this way, the narrator finds herself in the Hero Shima Diner—a real place in Hiroshima which I have creatively reimagined to house both a survivor tree and photos of hibakusha on the walls. The speaker-poet is asked by the diner's chef to write a poem for each of the survivors, in exchange for a meal. As she does so, she encounters a range of contemporary heroes in the diner and confronts earlier memories of a visit to Japan with her lover.

Works Cited

Campbell, Joseph 1998 *Power of Myth*, New York, NY: Doubleday.

Mecklin, John (ed) 2021 'This is your COVID wake-up call: It is 100 seconds to midnight', 2021 Doomsday Clock Statement, Science and Security Board Bulletin of the Atomic Scientists, 27 January: https://thebulletin.org/doomsday-clock/current-time/

Paul Munden

The term 'celebrity' first referred to a person in 1831 (OED). The word 'influencer' was coined even earlier, in the 1600s, but it was not until 2016 that it took on its modern connotation. I admit to discovering it only this year, squirming at its ugliness. There is now, apparently, 'a UK union for influencers, The Creator Union' (The Week 2021).

A number of these poems are based on incidents reported in the news. (Much googling was involved in my research and I dread to think how my search history appears as a result.) Others are an amalgamation of social media traits of the worst order—mixed with other widespread views, mostly abhorrent but not exclusively so; there is no absolute divide between moderately biased and seriously bigoted thinking.

Reflecting on poetic influences, the work of Peter Reading comes to mind as poetry that has 'resolutely refused to ignore areas of experience which in the opinion of many are beyond the treatment of Art. He himself has remarked: "Art has always struck me most when it was to do with ... things that are difficult to take"...' (Reading 1986: back cover). Reading examined deplorable social impoverishment with scathing humour, and I now know first-hand how difficult it is to walk that line. The plain box of prose poetry has helped me deliver what I cannot imagine in any other poetic form.

As for the speaker of these poems, his 'facts' are not too well grounded. We have witnessed the vilification of Media Studies (Wright 2020), but it strikes me that the subject is more important now than ever, if we are to negotiate the tone and purpose—and sometimes sheer deceit—in the words and other signs we encounter in various contexts. Poetry, and its study, should surely assist. In *The Bulmer Murder* (2017), I considered the notion of the writer as accomplice to the depicted crime. In this new sequence, I take an opposite approach, using a persona and vicious satire to forge a misalignment. I feel that Hesiod's concept of an utterly debased age calls for poems that probe the diseased thinking that lurks within our world. In case anyone is in doubt (as with some viewers needing to be told that *The Crown* is not a documentary), these selfies are a deceit: they are not mine (and some, even, are clearly fake within the fictional world of their speaker). Nevertheless, I hope they are in some appalling way believable. Indeed, I am convinced that many of the viewpoints presented are at large in the darker corners of our society, alongside things much worse. There is a suggestion, at the end of the sequence, that there may be causes for the character's depraved attitudes; I find this discomforting—both as an excuse for the inexcusable and as an indicator of a legacy of abuse, but there it is. It may also be controversial to be suggestive of remorse, though I believe it is something to hope for.

In asking myself hard questions about the 'right' I have to call out 'wrongs', something that might better be done by those abused, I answer that animals slaughtered for sport have no such opportunity; etc. The targets of the satire are the so-called human beings who seek to gain social capital through selfish and abhorrent acts, unconcerned how fame or fortune is amassed; in one poem, the speaker talks glibly of people not batting an eyelid at his behaviour. My instinct in writing these poems is to be nothing if not alert to the difficult truth of attitudes present within a society we prefer to think civilised.

Works Cited

Munden, Paul 2017 *The Bulmer Murder*, Canberra: Recent Work Press

Reading, Peter 1986 *STET*, London: Secker & Warburg

The Week 2021 'The rise of the social media influencer', 20 May: https://www.theweek.co.uk/social-media/952891/social-media-influencer-rise

Wright, Mic 2020 'Why Tony Blair's forever war on Media Studies is still important', 6 July: https://brokenbottleboy.substack.com/p/why-tony-blairs-forever-war-on-media

About the Poets

CASSANDRA ATHERTON is an award-winning writer and scholar of prose poetry. She was a Visiting Scholar in English at Harvard University and a Visiting Fellow in Literature at Sophia University, Tokyo. Her most recent books of prose poetry are *Leftovers* (2020) and the co-written *Fugitive Letters* (2020). She has written extensively on the atomic bomb, both critically and creatively, and is currently working on a book of prose poetry on the Hiroshima maidens with funding from the Australia Council. Cassandra co-wrote *Prose Poetry: An Introduction* (Princeton, University Press, 2020) and co-edited the *Anthology of Australian Prose Poetry* (Melbourne University Press, 2020) with Paul Hetherington. She is co-host of the international poetry livestream reading series, *LitBalm*, and associate editor at MadHat Press (USA).

OZ HARDWICK is a European poet, photographer, occasional musician, and accidental academic, whose work has been widely published in international journals and anthologies. He has published nine full collections and chapbooks, including *Learning to Have Lost* (IPSI, 2018), which won the 2019 Rubery International Book Award for poetry, and most recently the prose poetry sequence *Wolf Planet* (Hedgehog, 2020). As a photographer, Oz has had work on many album covers, and as a musician he has played at Glastonbury as the Summer Solstice sun rose. None of this is as impressive as it sounds. Oz is Professor of English at Leeds Trinity University.

PAUL HETHERINGTON is a distinguished Australian poet and scholar who has published 16 full-length books of poetry and prose poetry and a verse novel, along with 11 poetry chapbooks. He has won or been nominated for over 30 national and international awards and competitions, most recently winning the 2021 Bruce Dawe National Poetry Prize. He is Professor of Writing at the University of Canberra, head of the International Poetry Studies Institute and joint founding editor of the journal *Axon: Creative Explorations*. He founded the International Prose Poetry Group and, with Cassandra Atherton, is co-author of *Prose Poetry: An Introduction* (Princeton University Press, 2020) and co-editor of *Anthology of Australian Prose Poetry* (Melbourne University Press, 2020).

PAUL MUNDEN is a poet, editor and screenwriter living in North Yorkshire. A Gregory Award winner, he has published five poetry collections, including *Chromatic* (UWA Publishing, 2017), with a sixth, *Amplitude*, to be published in 2022 by Recent Work Press. He is editor of various poetry anthologies, most recently *Divining Dante* (Recent Work Press, 2021). For the British Council he has covered a number of scientific and humanitarian themes as conference poet and edited the anthology, *Feeling the Pressure: Poetry and science of climate change* (British Council, 2008). He was director of the UK's National Association of Writers in Education, 1994-2018, and is now an Adjunct Associate Professor at the University of Canberra, Australia.

Jen Webb is Dean, Graduate Research, at the University of Canberra, and co-editor of the scholarly journal *Axon: Creative Explorations* and the literary journal, *Meniscus*. She researches creativity and culture, and publications include *Researching Creative Writing* (Frontinus, 2015), and *Art and Human Rights: Contemporary Asian Contexts* (with Caroline Turner; Manchester University Press, 2016). With Paul Hetherington she is co-editor of the bilingual (Mandarin/English) anthology *Open Windows: Contemporary* Australian Poetry (Shanghai Joint Publishing Company, 2016). Her recent poetry collections are *Moving Targets* (Recent Work Press, 2018) and, with Shé Hawke, *Flight Mode* (Recent Work Press, 2020).

IPSI: INTERNATIONAL POETRY STUDIES

International Poetry Studies (IPSI) is part of the Centre for Creative and Cultural Research, Faculty of Arts and Design, University of Canberra. IPSI conducts research related to poetry, and publishes and promulgates the outcomes of this research internationally. IPSI also publishes poetry and interviews with poets, as well as related material, from around the world. Publication of such material takes place in IPSI's online journal *Axon: Creative Explorations* (www.axonjournal.com.au) and through other publishing vehicles. IPSI's goals include working—collaboratively, where possible—for the appreciation and understanding of poetry, poetic language and the cultural and social significance of poetry. IPSI also organises symposia, seminars, readings and other poetry related activities and events.

CCCR: CENTRE FOR CREATIVE AND CULTURAL RESEARCH

The Centre for Creative and Cultural Research (CCCR) is IPSI's umbrella organisation and brings together staff, adjuncts, research students and visiting fellows who work on key challenges within the cultural sector and creative field. A central feature of its research concerns the effects of digitisation and globalisation on cultural producers, whether individuals, communities or organisations.

Printed in Australia
AUHW020938081021
353354AU00006B/15